W9-BYZ-644

FIT *from* WITHIN

FIT *from* WITHIN

101 *Simple Secrets to Change Your Body*

and Your Life—

Starting Today and Lasting Forever

Victoria Moran

Contemporary Books

Chicago   New York   San Francisco   Lisbon   London   Madrid   Mexico City
Milan   New Delhi   San Juan   Seoul   Singapore   Sydney   Toronto

The **McGraw·Hill** Companies

Library of Congress Cataloging-in-Publication Data

Moran, Victoria, 1950–
      Fit from within : 101 simple secrets to change your body and your life—
   starting today and lasting forever / Victoria Moran.
         p.   cm.
      Includes bibliographical references (p.).
      ISBN 0-07-138426-X (hardcover)
      ISBN 0-07-141260-3 (paperback)
      1. Weight loss.   2. Weight loss—Psychological aspects.   I. Title.

   RM222.2.M5678   2002
   613.7—dc21   2001054763

Copyright © 2002 by Victoria Moran. All rights reserved. Printed in the United States
of America. Except as permitted under the United States Copyright Act of 1976, no
part of this publication may be reproduced or distributed in any form or by any
means, or stored in a database or retrieval system, without the prior written
permission of the publisher.

3 4 5 6 7 8 9 0   LBM/LBM   2 1 0 9 8 7 6 5 4 3

ISBN 0-07-138426-X (hardcover)
ISBN 0-07-141260-3 (paperback)

Interior design by Monica Baziuk

McGraw-Hill books are available at special quantity discounts to use as premiums
and sales promotions, or for use in corporate training programs. For more information, please write to the Director of Special Sales, Professional Publishing, McGraw-
Hill, Two Penn Plaza, New York, NY 10121-2298. Or contact your local bookstore.

This book is intended as a reference only, not as a medical manual. The information
given here is designed to help you make informed decisions about your health. It is
not a substitute for any treatment or practice that may have been prescribed or recommended by your doctor. If you suspect that you have a medical problem, seek
competent medical help.

This book is printed on acid-free paper.

To PATTI, for giving me a life's work,
a medium for my mission,
and continued inspiration that
one person can do a world of good.

ALSO BY VICTORIA MORAN

Body Confident: A Guided Journal for Losing Weight and Feeling Great

My Yoga Journal: Guided Reflections Through Writing

Lit from Within: Tending Your Soul for Lifelong Beauty

Creating a Charmed Life: Sensible, Spiritual Secrets Every Busy Woman Should Know

Shelter for the Spirit: Create Your Own Haven in a Hectic World

Contents

PREFACE

IF YOU WANT A HEALTHIER relationship with food and your body, or if you want to lose weight for the last time instead of just another time, I think I can help you. Whether overeating and overweight are minor annoyances for you or oppressive obstacles keeping the life you want to live out of reach, there are suggestions in this book for you. If some of the references—to binge eating or food addiction, for instance—don't apply to you, skip over them. If you're well acquainted with them, that's fine, too. So was I.

Reaching a stable weight that is reasonable, healthy, and attractive *for you* requires a transformation in the way you think and the way you live so you're free to make wise choices. If your life stays the way it is now, your weight will get back to where it is now in spite of your best intentions. Changing on the inside is the key to making outer changes last.

The attitudes and actions I recommend will, if you take them to heart, result in the kind of weight loss that will get you through the rough and tumble: pregnancy, nursing, and birthday parties;

vacations and changes of season; good days, bad days, and holidays; employment and unemployment; love and loss; PMS and menopause; injury, illness, grief, glory, agitation, celebration, and the rest.

If you heed these suggestions, you will lose weight, keep it off, and stop worrying about food and the state of your body. I can make this statement because worries about food and my body—out-of-control eating, crash diets, sensible diets, losing weight, gaining weight, shame, guilt, deprivation, and despair—colored much of my life for thirty-three years. The past eighteen have been different because of what I'm about to share with you. As you apply these principles in ways that make sense to you, you will be able to replace watching your weight with fully living your life. Believe me, it is a magnificent trade.

ACKNOWLEDGMENTS

IF IT TAKES A VILLAGE to raise a child, it takes at least a neighborhood to bring a book into being. For this one, I owe sincere thanks to my editor, Matthew Carnicelli, who recognized the importance of these ideas from the outset; his assistant, Michele Pezzuti, who has offered valuable insights and suggestions; and all the other capable people at Contemporary Books–McGraw-Hill who have contributed their expertise to this project.

I am, of course, extremely grateful to my family: my husband, William Melton, who believes in my work and supports my dreams more than I could ever have imagined or expected; my daughter, Adair Moran, who provided the wonderful insights of a young woman who, even in the intensely appearance-oriented world of acting, has exceptionally good sense about food and weight; my stepchildren, Siân Melton, Erik Melton, and James Melton, who, like William and Adair, made sacrifices to help me get this book finished on time; and my mother, Gladys Marshall, who gives me a vision of what it is to stay fit, vibrant, and plucky through every stage of life.

As with every book I write, I am grateful to Patti Breitman, my literary agent, champion, and confidante; my foreign rights agent, Linda Michaels, and her staff, who give my books an audience around the world; my computer guru, Pete Shiflett; and the reference librarians at the Kansas City, Missouri, Public Library. (I thought that with the Internet I wouldn't need them anymore. Wrong.)

I wish to thank Jane Murray, M.D., my physician and friend, who provided valuable information on the medical aspects of weight loss; and friends, colleagues, and supporters, including Arlynn Greenbaum, Marty Kraft, Jay Mulvaney, Reverend Duke Tufty, and all the rest of you who have been there with information, assistance, and a listening ear. Thanks also to everyone who works at the "remote offices" where I wrote this book: Annedore's, Muddy's, and the Supreme Bean coffeehouses in Kansas City, Missouri, and the Starbucks at 86th and Columbus in New York City.

Finally, thanks to the generous people who took time from their busy schedules to read the manuscript and give *Fit from Within* their endorsement; the faithful readers who let me know that I am indeed practicing right livelihood in doing what I do; and, most of all, the many people who have shared their healing from food addiction and weight obsession with me over the years. You are angels in my life. There is no way I can thank you enough.

INTRODUCTION

My Story

I KEEP A DOG-EARED, black-and-white picture of myself that was taken at my second birthday party. In it, I am lunging for the cake. For the next thirty-one years, I continued to lunge at food—preferably the sweet, sticky kinds, but salty and cheesy and creamy would do.

There was time off, of course, for dieting. My mother was slender and beautiful, but she had been a fat child and wanted to save me from the shame she had endured, so she educated me about diets and calories. My father, a physician with a sizable weight control clientele, brought home every new diet he learned about at conferences and from drug company detail men. I hated the diets—the silly ones and the scientific ones, the ones that made me hungry and the ones that made me bored. I vowed that when I got old enough I would never diet again.

Instead, once puberty hit, I put myself on more diets and more rigorous ones than my parents ever had. I fasted—fourteen and eighteen and twenty-three days, on nothing but water. I joined diet clubs and lost the weight but was too afraid of regaining it to try some kind of maintenance plan, so I stayed on the diet and once got down to ninety-one pounds. Nobody labeled it anorexia, because I was eating. More than eating: I was stuffing myself into bloated oblivion on cauliflower and leaf lettuce and a nasty confection called *coffee whip*, a dessert made of instant coffee, unflavored gelatin, and Sweet & Low. When I couldn't take it anymore, I went back to eating what I really wanted in the same quantities that I had been eating diet food. Within six months I'd doubled my weight, and instead of being dangerously thin I was once again predictably fat.

Although food was my nemesis, I believed it could also be my salvation. I studied nutrition. I became a health writer. I figured if I learned enough, I would act on what I knew. I didn't. I lived part-time. When I was losing extra weight, or on those rare occasions when I lost all of it, I soaked up life like a person with only weeks to live. I figured that was what I had. I rarely kept weight off for more than a few weeks anyway.

I felt ecstatic when my weight was going down and desolate when it was going up. I hated myself for being fat, even though my top weight was only sixty-some pounds above normal for me, and I often agonized over being only fifteen to twenty pounds overweight. In spite of my never having a hundred pounds to lose, I had a hundred ways to abuse myself. I stole food from my grandmother's kitchen and the office galley. I spent my paycheck on junk food and a few times sold the postage stamps I had in my wallet to get the fifty cents I was short on bus fare. I invested my youth in diets, binges, and self-hatred.

One afternoon when I was thirty-three years old, married with a seven-month-old daughter, I handed the baby to her dad and took myself out for lunch. I had binged the day before, but that day I was dieting, so I ordered a chef's salad and iced tea. I paid with a credit card. Then it hit me: I wasn't working. My husband was in school. We were living on student loans and imagination, and I was charging lunch to our only credit card that hadn't maxed out. I had wanted to be alone and absorb myself in a meal more than I wanted to contribute to the security of my family. My lunch was exemplary. My life was a mess.

I went home and called a wise friend I knew had once been in the same sorry state I was in but who had found a way out. "I was hoping you would call," she said. "It's time for you to get over this." She told me to be willing for even one moment to give up the whole thing. The foods I depended on. The protected feeling I got from being fat. The heady pleasure of being thin. The sense of control that came from dieting. The aura of drama with which I could surround myself by going on binges and despising my body and my life. She told me to ask God or Jesus or Buddha or the massive oak tree outside my dining room window to give me the power I didn't have myself. And she told me I didn't have to do anything forever, just today.

That was eighteen years ago. I had a lot of work to do, but controlling my weight wasn't part of it. I'd never been able to have that kind of control, and I was finally willing to stop trying. Instead I focused on developing my spiritual life and on getting through each day without harming myself with food. I went back to the yoga classes I'd dropped out of and began to believe that I was acceptable, physically as well as spiritually. I lost weight without obsessing over losing weight. Through these eighteen years I have usually eaten exactly what I needed to be both satisfied and healthy. Sometimes I've eaten too much. The sky didn't fall, and I didn't gain weight. I realize now that nature really does cut us some slack. We don't have to be perfect, just willing. And honest. And able to trust—a Higher Power, the process of life, and, eventually, even ourselves.

During this time I have learned what it takes to stay slim and, more critically, what it takes to stay sane. I have learned to care for myself, find my place in the world, enjoy food, and enjoy life more. Almost no one who loses weight keeps it off for eighteen years. The statistics claim that only 2 percent of people who lose twenty-five pounds or more keep it off for even seven years, and two-thirds of all dieters regain their weight within twelve months. You do not have to be one of those statistics. Not anymore. You can experience what I have by adapting the suggestions in this book to your life, your circumstances, and your idea of how grace and good sense can join forces to generate a substantial change for the better.

I am convinced that I have not been given these years of freedom just because I'm one lucky woman. I believe I have had this privilege in order to share with you what made it happen. It's your turn now.

FIT *from* WITHIN

ACCEPT YOURSELF TODAY

If you don't accept yourself, you won't live fully, and if you

don't live fully, you'll need to get full some other way.

ACCEPTING WHO YOU ARE, body and soul, does not guarantee that you will lose weight. It does, however, put you in the ideal position for losing weight—not just one more time but for the last time. If you don't accept yourself, you won't live fully, and if you don't live fully, you'll need to get full some other way.

It can be hard to accept yourself if you're too heavy (or if you think you are), because the mass culture as it's printed and televised finds fat abhorrent. This leads to self-hatred, more eating, and less exercising ("I can't be seen in workout clothes. I'll exercise after I lose the first ten pounds").

You may not be consciously thinking, "I'm completely unacceptable today, but at 120 pounds I'll be perfect." Unconsciously, though, it's difficult not to have such thoughts, because the media bombards us with the message that only *thin* (and while we're at it, we may as well add *young*) bodies are acceptable.

Every age and culture has had its physical ideal, but only in recent history has that ideal been foisted on us hundreds of times a day through magazines, movies, and TV. The implication that even normal weight isn't thin enough makes it hard for a lot of people, women in particular, to accept and value themselves. If you *are* overweight, it's even harder.

The suggestion, subliminal or stated, that we should all have a supermodel's body is as preposterous as suggesting that we should all have Albert Einstein's IQ. If mathematical theorems were valued as highly in the mass culture as fashion spreads and celebrity profiles, we'd be lamenting the paucity of our intellects instead of the flabbiness of our thighs.

Get clear on this: being fat is not disgusting. Child abuse is disgusting. Tying up a dog outside all day and night in every kind of weather is disgusting. Homelessness and starvation and weapons of mass destruction are disgusting. Overweight is a state. A situation. An inconvenience certainly. A threat to health in many cases. A sign, perhaps, of self-indulgence or indifference or emotional distress. But not disgusting.

It is vital that you understand this at the outset. Otherwise you may at some future time be living blissfully as a size six, and something will happen. You might retain water before a period or react to some medicine with weight gain. Or perhaps you reach midlife and awaken one morning to find that some hormonal desperado fled in the night with your flat tummy and left you a round one instead. Unless you come to accept yourself the way you are every day, shifts like these could send you back into "disgusting" mode, the ideal place for regaining all your lost weight. Acceptance, on the other hand, does double duty. It gives you peace of mind in the present and makes change possible for the future.

Acceptance is not rationalizing overeating as okay. Nothing that is diminishing your life belongs in your life, whether that's an abusive boss, an untreated illness, or a peculiar affinity for layer cake and leftovers. Your behavior around food is a—you pick the word—habit, weakness, sickness, raw deal. Whatever you call it, it's something in which you participate; it's not who you are. Deal with the problem, but accept yourself.

2

HONOR WHO YOU ARE

⌒

You can eat better and still be yourself.

YOU CAN ADOPT BETTER habits only if they honor who you are: your ethnicity, religion, and lifestyle, the climate where you live, the hours you work, and the stage of life you're in. When I worked for a large commercial diet program (before I doubled my weight and embarrassed everybody), a lot of the participants in my area were first-generation Hispanic women. Every week when I described the food program (I wasn't supposed to call it a diet, but it was), one of the Latinas would ask, "What about tortillas?" I would say, "They're not on the program." Week after week the tortilla question would come up, and week after week the majority of the Latin women didn't come back a second time. Meals without tortillas made no sense to them.

I remembered this years later after I realized that I simply wasn't able to diet anymore. I'd spent so long eating by other people's standards—my dad's, the diet doctors', the weight loss organizations'—that I had few standards left of my own. I had to find some, so I did a self-assessment. I wanted to be healthy—at least I knew that much—and I wanted to eat attractive, good-tasting food that I wouldn't regret having eaten afterward. This was enough to give me some boundaries: there were some foods I wouldn't eat but lots more that I would. And, unlike enduring all those diets, I was now making intelligent, adult choices about what I would eat. If my idea about what was healthy, attractive, and good tasting changed, I could change accordingly. I'd made some decisions, but I hadn't taken any pledges. I could eat better and still be myself.

You, too, can eat better and still be yourself. Authors, experts, and your mother-in-law all have their opinions. You need to have your own. Ask yourself:

- What does reasonable eating look like to me?

- How much time do I want to spend preparing food?

- What challenges to improving the way I eat does the work I do present?

- Do I need to allow for a lot of traveling and time away from home?

- Will my spouse or family be a help or a hindrance to my making these changes?

- Am I feeding children throughout the day?

- Do I have a health condition that requires me to eat in a certain way?

- Are there religious or ethical or cultural proscriptions about food that I want to hold to for myself?

For almost everybody, dieting is unnatural and unrealistic, but unless you're incarcerated and have no say at all about the food provided, there *is* a healthy, satisfying way of eating that is natural and realistic for you. The point is to know yourself, respect yourself, and make appropriate choices based on who you are and how you live. When you make the alterations that will change your body and your life, they have to be ones that work for you and that honor who you are. The point is to have a trimmer body and a healthier lifestyle, not to reincarnate as somebody else.

Include a Spiritual Component

I eat differently and I exercise more consistently than I used to,

but I wouldn't be able to do either of those things if my heart

and soul had not undergone extensive repairs.

PEOPLE WITH HEAVY-DUTY food problems—we'll talk about those in Chapter 20—almost invariably need the kind of antiaddiction program that includes a strong spiritual component. The difference between success and failure—and sometimes even life and death—is how fully they can turn their lives over to the care of the God of their understanding. Even if you're not in this serious league, you will benefit if you, too, include a spiritual component in your quest for a lifetime of healthy eating and comfortable weight.

In my own case a spiritual turnaround is responsible for my having been free from overeating for eighteen years. Yes, I eat differently and I exercise more consistently than I used to, but I wouldn't be able to do either of those things if my heart and soul had not undergone extensive repairs. I wasn't fat because of ignorance about calories and abdominal crunches. I was fat because I had deified food, expecting it to comfort me, console me, and get me through life. I suppose it did, after a fashion, but it wasn't the life I wanted or the life I deserved.

If you feel that you deserve a better life than you're currently living—whether only where food and weight are concerned or in other areas, too—please open your mind to the possibility that a spiritual component may have been the active ingredient lacking in your previous efforts. It is, in fact, the key element that separates becoming fit from within from just losing weight again.

One way to see the spiritual component in this is to realize that there is more to who you are than your body, intellect, and emotions. Your *higher* or *deeper* or *real* self is that spiritual part of you, your essence. When you keep it in mind, you're more likely to live healthfully and eat moderately, both because you'll value yourself more and because you'll have something besides your human willpower to depend on.

Going even deeper, having a spiritual component is absolutely necessary if you believe you've done all you can to get a grip on the food issue and it seems to get harder, not easier, over time. If you can't do this yourself, give yourself a break and turn to something that can. If you don't believe in God, pretend. Anybody who has been able to make a god out of a snack cake can certainly envision someone who gave you the stars and the seasons, your son and your daughter.

The people I know who maintain weight losses indefinitely and without anxiety have, in whatever way fits their own religious and philosophical sense of things, surrendered their eating and weight issues to some Higher Power. This is not the same as promising

God you'll never overeat again, nor is it making deals, begging and pleading, or acting pitiful in hopes of receiving divine pity. (If you've done those things, you know how poorly they work.)

Instead, including a spiritual component is simply knowing when you're up against something that is too much for you and your best intentions to handle on your own. It's realizing where you're weak and depending on something strong, whether you think of that as God in heaven or a power that, although beyond your human ego, resides inside yourself.

If you only need to lose some weight but food has not bullied you into a place of hopelessness and despair, you may not need to surrender in this way at all. But I've never known anyone to regret it. For some, this simply takes the pressure off. For others, it makes beating this thing possible when it never was before.

4

As a Rule, Eat Three Meals a Day

If you start to eat only three times, you have to stop only

three times, and stopping has been the problem.

MY EXPERIENCE AND observations have convinced me that the majority of people who have trouble with weight do best with three meals a day as a general rule. The rationale behind three meals a day is simple: if you start to eat only three times, you have to stop only three times, and stopping has been the problem.

Besides, society is set up for three meals a day, thus the "bed and breakfast," the "lunch special," the "dinner date." When you're on this schedule, too, you fit in nicely with the world you live in and the people around you. This doesn't mean there can never be an exception, that you will never have afternoon tea or an after-theater snack or popcorn at the movies. Nothing that you eat rationally and out of choice rather than compulsion will interfere with the fit-from-within process. Nevertheless, I highly recommend that, unless you have a medical condition that requires you to eat more often, you stick with three meals a day most of the time.

If you do, there will be several waking hours during which you will have nothing in your mouth. This is good. This is when you learn to focus on your inner life and your outer world instead of on food. It's also when you come to know at a visceral level that, although food and water and air are indispensable for maintaining your body, the essential individual that you are is sustained by something else, something more. This is a power that you can think of as God or as the life force you may know as *prana* if you've practiced yoga or as *chi* if you're familiar with martial arts.

Eating three meals a day is both a discipline and a gift. In the beginning, it might take all the fortitude you've got to get from one meal to the next without picking up something to eat. Call on your inner resources, understanding friends, or reading this book or something else that inspires you. Learn the difference between what it feels like to *be* hungry and to *think* you're hungry because you're used to eating often. Don't skip meals, either. You want to establish a nice, comfortable rhythm.

One more thing: should your food get out of hand—e.g., you eat something you can't possibly rationalize as appropriate or even if you go on an all-out binge—immediately return to three meals a day. The temptation is to say, "I overate yesterday, so today I won't eat at all," or "I'll skip breakfast and lunch and start over at dinner." Don't. Get back to your three-meals-a-day schedule as soon as you realize what happened. You don't have to eat a lot, but go through the motions. Sit down. Have a meal or part of one. Engage in conversation. In other words, reinforce this better habit both when things are going well and if they temporarily fall apart.

5

IN THE BEGINNING, EAT OUT

Go to a restaurant, enjoy your meal, and get on with your life.

RESTAURANTS HAVE GOTTEN a bad rap for serving only rich food and massive portions. But for anyone whose eating has been out of control, restaurant meals—generous servings and all—at least have limits. You order, the food comes to your table, you eat, pay, and leave. This eliminates the lure of second helpings, clearing off a child's plate, and knowing there is nothing but a refrigerator door between you and what's left of the mashed potatoes.

One caveat here: I said "restaurants," not fast-food places (see Chapter 76). Much of what is sold there will not build the kind of cellular structure that will help you become fit from within. Besides, the idea is to go out to eat. Make it as nice as you can.

That said, your job is to go to a restaurant, enjoy your meal, and get on with your life. Do this for a day or two—or even for a month if it takes that long to get you comfortable eating a meal that doesn't go on all day and night. Even a brief hiatus from eating at home can do wonders. You won't have to cook, clean up, or put away leftovers until you feel surer of yourself. You'll get valuable practice in making healthier choices, both when you select a restaurant and when you order from the menu. And by being aware that you're sometimes getting more food than you need and other times perhaps not quite enough, you'll get a sense of what a moderate meal looks like and how it feels to eat one.

Eventually, you'll get really good at knowing when you've had enough. Then you'll leave food on your plate or take what you didn't finish tonight home for tomorrow's lunch. This will happen in time. For now, eat all you want, even if that's every morsel. If you're at a salad bar or buffet, commit to going through the line just once (use two plates if they're small). You don't get extra points for skimping. What is vital is imprinting on your psyche how it feels to eat a meal that has a definite beginning and a definite end.

At this point, skip the doggy bag unless you actually have a dog. You don't want the temptation of having to think about something heavenly in Styrofoam. You're training yourself now to eat when it's time to eat and live when it's time to live.

6

FOCUS ON LIVING A QUALITY LIFE

Put all the energy, emphasis, and willpower you used to

spend going on diets and hating your hips into

increasing the quality of your life.

EVERYBODY HAS EXPERIENCED being so involved in a project that a mealtime passes unnoticed—maybe even two mealtimes. It would be unrealistic to expect that level of involvement in every moment. Besides, you'd starve to death. That *quality* of involvement, however, needs to be with you all the time. If your life is boring or not fulfilling or unsuited to the person you are, it's no wonder you eat too much. You're lucky you're not doing something worse.

Going on a diet is the most foolish move you can make if you're in this place of life deprivation. A diet would only deprive you more and make things worse. Instead, make your life richer. Start with small things: a more attractive environment at home, at work, even in your car. Treat yourself better. Sleep in decent nightclothes instead of old T-shirts. Take a bath every day and put bath salts or bubbles or fragrant oil in the water.

And eat better food. I'm not talking about diet food, just better food—food you'd feed the president if he were coming to dinner, assuming that you voted for him, of course. Think attractive food. Good-tasting food. Quality food. Fresh produce is quality food. Whole grains are quality food. An exquisite meal at a restaurant where the tablecloth is actually made of cloth is quality food. Surprisingly perhaps, even one lovely piece of pricey chocolate can be quality food. Chocolate is rather like sex, which can run the gamut from a sacred experience to a criminal act. If you're going to eat chocolate, have the kind you'd take home to meet your parents. You're not likely to find it in a vending machine.

Start to recognize quality food. Eating it will build higher-quality tissues in your body, which will in turn bring higher-quality experiences to your life. Try to see it this way: your body/mind processes information and stimuli from the outside world. It tends to attract stimuli that are on its own wavelength—like when you learn the definition of a word you didn't know before, and it seems that everywhere you turn somebody is saying *nonplussed* or *perspicacity*. When it comes to your body and brain, the superior cells you create by eating high-quality food evoke superior perceptions. Simple as that.

Recognize low-quality food, too, and avoid it whenever you can. Take this approach with every other aspect of your days and nights. You are a goddess (gentlemen: Adonis). Treat yourself as such—even if you have been known to fall asleep on the couch with unbrushed teeth and clutching what's left of the package of sandwich cookies.

Commit yourself to living a quality life. Put all the energy, emphasis, and willpower you used to spend going on diets and hating your hips into increasing the quality of your life. Take advantage of all that is offered to you today—as long as it's legal, moral, and appeals to your best self. Don't miss a chance to experience beauty or have an adventure. Fill yourself with wonder so you don't have to fill yourself with so much dinner. You deserve a quality life. Good food will be part of it, but not nearly the best part.

7

GIVE UP THE NOTION
OF BLOWING IT

When you cannot blow it—even by eating too much—the times

when you do overeat will become fewer and fewer.

THE SIMPLE SENTENCE "I blew it" may be responsible for more weight gained than all the French fries at McDonald's. The scenario is, "I ate a [cookie, potato chip, candy bar]. I blew it. So now I have to eat for three days and be really miserable." Remember: there is nothing to blow. You are not on a diet. You had a cookie. Fine. I hope it tasted good. I hope you left some in the bag for somebody else. Either way, it's done. Get your brain out of your palate and go do something interesting.

The *blowing it* concept is a setup. It's a mind game overeaters play to give themselves permission to eat for a fix. If you blow it, you have to throw in the towel. Give up. Wallow in remorse. Then you have to face the daunting prospect of starting over: a new diet, another exercise regimen, another monumental undertaking.

Instead, don't blow it. There are two ways to accomplish this. One is to keep your expectations realistic so you will reach them. For example, aspiring to eat three reasonable meals today and take a walk in the morning is realistic. Setting your sites on running five miles a day and eating nothing but skinless chicken and lettuce leaves for the next six weeks isn't.

The other way to stop blowing it is to disallow the concept itself. Let's say your plan today is to walk and eat three moderate meals, but you overslept, didn't walk, and had a lunch that would have been moderate for an NFL lineman but not for you. Did you blow it? No—unless you want to get back on the diet-and-binge merry-go-round. Instead, face the facts of what happened, eat a moderate dinner, and take a walk afterward.

I had been free from bingeing and despising myself for about four months when I went out for a pizza dinner. I figured I'd have salad and two, maybe three, slices of pizza. When the pizza showed up, it was "Chicago style"—cut into little squares and rectangles of varying sizes, instead of the dependable triangles I'd expected. I ate what seemed like two or three slices, but when the meal was over and I stood up and felt my stomach pressing on my waistband, I knew I'd eaten quite a bit more.

My modus operandi up to that point had always been, "You blew it. For shame! You can't do anything right," followed by a binge of several weeks or more. That night, however, it was as if I had acquired a wise counselor within myself who suggested an entirely different response: "Yeah, you ate a lot. Sometimes that will happen. Let it go." So I did. That single act altered a negative pattern I'd had all my life.

When you cannot blow it—even by eating too much—the times when you do overeat will become fewer and fewer. You'll spend less time on remorse and more on fulfillment.

8

SLOW DOWN AND SIT DOWN

Begin by slowing down and sitting down for your meals. Then let yourself slow down and be more fully present for your life.

THE FRENCH ARE SLIMMER than Americans in spite of their butter and sauces and pastries. Researchers who have looked into this phenomenon have concluded that the primary reason for this is that the French know how to slow down and sit down. Meals are events for them, and cuisine is an art form to be savored.

When you eat on the run, your body and brain have a hard time realizing that you ate at all. They're expecting an *experience*, the ritual of dining, not just some food thrown down the hatch. Give your physical and mental selves what they're desiring: some time set aside for the meal. Cooking smells from the kitchen. Washing up for dinner and maybe even changing your clothes to alert yourself to the fact that something civilized is about to happen. Sit down at a table and have a place setting: nothing fancy required, just something inviting. Put on music. Light a candle. You may be feeling more relaxed by just reading these words and imagining this scene. Think how content you'll feel when you turn it into reality.

Everyone is busy, and having three formal meals a day is out of the question for most of us. Can you at least *sit* for every meal, even the less-than-leisurely ones? Can you leave your desk at lunchtime or, if that's not possible, shift gears, set your work aside, and look at a magazine or a catalog instead of at work stuff while you eat? Can you take steps to retrieve dinner from its hurried, everybody-is-going-a-different-direction pattern and reinvent it as something special, if only a couple of nights a week?

When you slow down and sit down, you'll taste your food. You'll experience culinary pleasures that take some time to sink in. You'll actually give your brain the twenty minutes it's supposed to need to register that you have indeed eaten. Slowing down for meals is also good training in slowing down for other things.

Although I'm better at this general slowing down than I used to be, I fall short on remembering that I can take my time, approach one activity at a time, and not miss something. I was multitasking before I'd ever heard the word, and a lot of times it's gotten me into trouble. For example, I turn on bath water and then go off and wash dishes, pick up phone messages, and answer E-mail. That's not so bad at my house in Kansas City, where the tub has a runoff drain, but when I had a temporary apartment in New York that lacked that amenity, I flooded the bathroom—and the downstairs apartment—*twice*.

Each time the consequences were swift and severe: having to lug thirty pounds of dripping towels to the 110-degree launderette, where I was chastised in several languages for assorted breaches of Launderama etiquette. That should have taught me, right? But the conventional wisdom about learning from mistakes won't hold up without the willingness to do it. I have to be willing to slow down, to spend three and a half minutes in the bathroom waiting for the tub to fill, and do nothing else except tweeze my eyebrows or wipe out the basin or indulge in an abridged daydream. Filling the bathtub this way, and conducting the rest of my life in similar fashion, adds to the serenity I have stored up. Serenity is insurance against eating like crazy and doing other crazy things, too.

The stress that invites overeating is cumulative. Because I have more serenity than stress today, my periodic lapses send me only to the launderette, not to the candy store. Still, it is a grace to be able to answer someone's "Do you have a minute?" with "For you, certainly." It is a blessing to be able to read a novel and not feel guilty about the time it took. It's even nice to sit long enough for your nails to dry so you don't have to swear, repair a smudge, and start over. I would like more of those easy times, and perhaps you would, too. Begin by slowing down and sitting down for your meals. Then let yourself slow down and be more fully present for your life.

9

Eat like a Healthy Human Being

~

Dieting is the backside of binge eating. They travel together.

You can do without both in your life.

EAT LIKE A HEALTHY human being. In other words, swear off dieting. By whatever name you call it, dieting is both depressing and counterproductive. Diets create overweight by tricking the body into believing there is a famine in the land and every calorie is precious. Besides, deprived people overeat when the period of deprivation is up—even those who have never had a weight problem and have rarely overeaten before.

Alter the cycle by eating like a healthy human being instead of a sanitarium patient on a prescribed and monitored diet. Start with the resolve that you are finished with diets but you are willing to exercise some restraint. This is the middle path. It is not sexy and exciting, nor is it agonizing and dramatic. For this reason, it has never been widely popular in the "Hey, have we got something new for you!" world of weight control. Nevertheless, it works.

Although it is a gentle approach, it does take some mettle. It's easy to think, "If I weigh 160 *with* dieting, I'd probably be 260 without it." Draw on your courage and my history to convince yourself that dieting is simply the backside of binge eating. They travel together. You can do without both in your life. You can employ the mind-set of eating like a healthy human being even if there are guidelines to which you must adhere because of a health problem. Look at these as aids to your eating like a healthy human being.

People who have dieted for a long time get so used to it that they're uncomfortable doing anything else. They feel unprotected, overwhelmed by choices and temptations. If you feel this way, take refuge in knowing that giving up dieting does not mean open season at the food court. Remember: you're committed to eating like a healthy human being.

Do some thinking about what this means to you. How do healthy, rational, confident human beings nourish themselves? What kinds of foods do they prefer? How much? Do they deprive and berate themselves about what they eat? What do these people do about social functions that involve food? Go over these questions seriously. Write answers to them in your notebook or journal (see Chapter 15). When you do so, you'll be writing your own prescription for a healthy life as far as eating is concerned.

Taking it one proverbial day at a time, resolve to eat like a healthy human being. If you run across a diet article in a magazine or a diet program on talk TV, turn the page or change the channel. You used to diet, and it helped make you fat. Now you're eating like a healthy human being instead.

10

IF IT DOESN'T LOOK GOOD,
DON'T EAT IT

Not every meal will be a gustatory adventure, nor does it have to be, but everything you put in your mouth does need to meet some basic standards.

OVERWEIGHT PEOPLE CAN be amazingly liberal in defining the word *edible*. We'll eat things other people simply wouldn't, both when we're on binges and when we're on diets. (Serious compulsive overeaters make the best short-term dieters. No one else could stomach all that celery or all those liquid meals made from corn syrup and hydrolyzed vegetable protein.) A hard-core overeater on a binge will chew and swallow just about anything: unthawed frozen food, stale pizza foraged from the trash can, leftovers that were left for far too long.

But even garden-variety overeaters can be pretty democratic about what they consume. Some genuinely believe that airline food is tasty, even in coach. Others will eat a dish that's too hot or too cold, overcooked or undercooked, or something they just don't like. They give food so many chances, taking bite after bite of this scalding/freezing/burned/raw/bad-tasting dish, as if eating enough of it could transform it into something good after all. When this fails to transpire, they rationalize with sentiments on the order of "This is my lunch; it's all I'll get," or "I'm paying for this; I'm darn well going to eat it."

To become fit from within, you have to develop discernment. This means becoming selective about what you put in your mouth—"picky" even. If you're at a restaurant and your entrée is charred black or still frozen in the middle, send it back. If your salad is basically okay but has a couple of pieces of brown lettuce, eat around those. This is what people who don't have weight problems do as a matter of course. They stopped cleaning their plate at age eleven when they figured out that, with skillful sleight of hand, they could slip the offending morsel to the dog and accept Mom's approving soliloquy: "Good for you, Julia. I knew you'd like liver if you'd just try it with an open mind."

Use this image: the meal before you is a pristine forest. The overeater's way of approaching it is clear-cutting—death and destruction as far as the eye can see. The normal eater's approach is like a child exploring the forest, determined to collect only the prettiest flowers, the most colorful leaves, and the truly interesting rocks in her basket.

Not every meal will be a gustatory adventure, nor does it have to be, but everything you put in your mouth does need to meet some basic standards. At the very least, it should be fresh, properly prepared, and taste like something. You're worth it.

11

To Weigh Less, Weigh Less

~

That number on the scale is a woefully imperfect indicator of

either the state of your health or the quality of your life.

I KEEP AN OLD BATHROOM scale on a closet shelf to weigh the box when I send something UPS. Otherwise I have no use for scales. They can make people crazy. When they indicate lost weight, it can be an invitation to say "Eat! Celebrate! Pull out all the stops!" When the message is gained weight, a common response is "I really screwed up this time. I may as well eat everything in sight."

There are plenty of people who never weigh themselves and do just fine. Those of us who have had weight problems tend to be sensitive to our girth, and unless we're in a state of binge-induced denial, we're pretty good at knowing whether our weight is going up, coming down, or remaining stable. The way clothes fit is another reliable indicator. Having to move over a belt notch—in either direction—tells us something, but without the horror or elation the same news might carry if it came from a scale.

Not weighing also puts the emphasis where it belongs, on living well, not tracking numbers. Just as some of the world's eternally youthful people pay no attention to their age, the naturally thin rarely know—or care—exactly how much they weigh.

Besides, studies abound that suggest that overweight people who exercise regularly can be healthier than normal-weight people who don't. And a fit, muscular person can weigh more than a fat, flabby person of the same height and bone structure. That number on the scale is a woefully imperfect indicator of either the state of your health or the quality of your life.

In spite of the potential pitfalls of weighing our bodies like deli meat, most of us do want to know how much we weigh. Some people believe that weighing on a regular, but not obsessive, basis keeps them honest. Your weight is also a piece of information about yourself that you have every right to know, like your blood type, your resting heart rate, and your cholesterol level.

I have found that weighing only once a month at the health club, the doctor's office, or some other neutral place is a reasonable compromise between weighing all the time and denying reality. This way you're on a scale that's more accurate than most of the ones people have at home and, unless you're a big UPS shipper, you don't have to be plagued by the presence of a weighing machine at all. If you're in the losing process, weighing once a month also allows time for something to actually happen, so you don't have to anguish over the daily fluctuations that are natural and normal.

If you know from experience that weighing is traumatic for you, regardless of where you do it or how often, save yourself the grief. When your doctor insists on a routine weigh-in, ask to face away from the scale. Be sure the nurse is capable of writing the number on your chart without announcing it like a late-breaking news story. That number is your business, and if you don't care to hear it, the rest of the world certainly doesn't need to.

12

GET HONEST ABOUT WHAT YOU EAT

If you are a closet eater, it is critical that you get out.

You accomplish this by eating in the open and saving

your closet for clothes.

KNOWING WHAT YOU WEIGH is optional. Knowing what you eat is essential. You've heard the lament and you may even have uttered it: "I don't know why I can't lose weight. I hardly eat anything." Mysteries do exist, and anybody who can maintain obesity and "hardly eat anything" is one of them. To this rare person I offer sympathy. To the rest of us I say, "Oh, for heaven's sake."

When I was dating my first husband, I was carrying 170 pounds on a delicate 5′5″ frame. I once overheard him telling his brother that he knew I must have some glandular problem since I never ate anything except cottage cheese and cantaloupe. It was true; I never ate anything but "diet food" in public. Alone, however, I was the ingenue that devoured Chicago. Even then I had the vague suspicion that if I could ever bring myself to eat an ice cream sundae or a piece of chocolate cake *in his presence*, some miracle might happen. That was my intuition letting me know how valuable honesty about my eating would one day become.

It's absurd to try to hide overeating since it shows on your body. If you try to outwit nature by vomiting or using laxatives or overexercising, that will show on your face. You'll look haggard, tired, older than you are. So stop trying to hide, by either innocuous means or potentially deadly ones. Instead, be honest with yourself about what you eat. Writing down your food (see Chapter 15) is one tool to help with that. Another is being part of a support group (see Chapter 42) where you can safely share with other people and not fear recrimination. Most helpful of all is to get into the habit of eating what you choose to eat, no matter who is present.

After a while you'll choose only what's best for you in almost every instance. In the meantime, be honest with yourself about what is going into your mouth and eat with as much integrity as you can. This may mean having to field insensitive remarks from people who think they have the right to oversee your food intake. They might ask, "Is that on your diet?" or "Should you really be eating that?" Try not to punch anybody (even if they deserve it) and eat what you need to eat now so you won't feel obliged to have twice as much later.

Don't worry that this might be slowing down your weight loss. If you're in this for keeps, you're willing to take your time. You realize that you have to change the way you think and the way you see yourself every bit as much as changing the foods you eat. If you are a closet eater, it is critical that you get out. You accomplish this by eating in the open and saving your closet for clothes. Do this courageously and consistently, and those clothes will eventually come in smaller sizes.

13

WALK MORE

~

Walking allows you to think, come up with solutions to problems, understand yourself better, and tap into insights you may not have remembered you have.

AN EXERCISE PROGRAM, in spite of the many physical and emotional benefits it can impart, will backfire just like a diet if it's too much too soon. Instead, start by walking more. It will make a tremendous difference in your attitude, your appetite, and your weight.

My home is Kansas City, Missouri, but I'm in the process of relocating to New York City, where I already spend a lot of time. A few years ago a fitness magazine dubbed Kansas City "the second fattest city in America." It was a totally unscientific study (they did things like tallying the number of fast-food places against the number of gyms in the Yellow Pages), but it is true that when I go home I see more heavy people than I do in New York. The difference, I believe, is walking. When I was a little girl, Kansas City was urban and people walked. Now suburbia rules, and most people drive everywhere. New Yorkers walk: to the market, the post office, the subway station. Even my dog lost weight when she spent the winter in New York, because she went on walks instead of just going out in the yard.

This will happen for you, too. Walking will make you a more efficient metabolizer of food, a happier, more positive person, and a healthier one. What's more, when you become a walker you'll feel more independent, knowing that you can get where you're going under your own steam. You'll see more scenery since walking puts your environment up close and personal. You'll look more radiant because you'll be breathing outdoor air. You'll feel the quadriceps muscles in your thighs and notice more shapeliness in your calves. You will literally walk right into an elevated sense of well-being.

Walking can also help you know yourself better, because it causes you to be with yourself. Even if you're walking at a steady clip, the fact that you're getting where you're going via human power invites you to slow your overall approach to life down to a more humane pace. Without the urgency of driving in traffic or exercising to exhaustion, walking allows you to think, come up with solutions to problems, understand yourself better, and tap into insights you may not have remembered you have.

Get into the walking habit by walking more today. Today: that's *this* 24-hour period. The old park-at-the-far-edge-of-the-lot strategy is a good enough place to start. You can also park in the first empty place you pass on the street instead of driving around and around in search of something closer to where you're going. You can walk on your lunch hour, in the morning with your neighbor, or after dinner with your own true love. You can take the stairs or offer to pick up the mail or to get bread and milk and oranges at the corner store.

If you live where there is no corner store, walking may seem boring, but being part of your surroundings—whatever they are—while walking is one way to be fully alive, fully present. Immerse yourself in all there is to see, hear, and smell precisely where you find yourself today. Take it all in. If you're a social person, start a walking group—the more, the merrier. With enough members, the group won't fold because some people quit. A tiny tape player and headphones can keep you company, too, especially if you listen to books on tape. I've extended many a walk because I wanted to know what would happen in the next chapter.

14

REFRAIN FROM JUDGING
BY APPEARANCES

The less you judge other people by the way they look,

the less judged by others you will feel yourself.

OSCAR WILDE WROTE, "It is only shallow people who do not judge by appearances." Okay, Oscar, you had a brilliant wit and a marvelous way with words, but you're not living in the twenty-first century. Ours is a media-led culture that implies that appearance is just about everything. This makes it difficult to raise children who understand the value of character. It causes us to think twice before telling our kids "It's what's on the inside that matters," when we know that what's on the outside will play a role in their getting jobs, friends, dates, and even grades.

This appearance consciousness also makes it tough to say to ourselves, "You have as good a chance as the next person," when the hard, cold fact is, if you're not attractive by current standards, you may well have a harder row to hoe than someone else. You and I both know this isn't fair, and we also know it's the way of things, fair or not. Although neither of us as individuals can change the prevailing cultural climate, we can refuse to take part in the more damaging aspects of it. The task is to refrain, as much as you can being human and living in the world as it is, from judging by appearances. The payoff is the less you judge other people by the way they look, the less judged by others you will feel yourself.

Curiously, overweight people can be more prejudiced against other overweight people than thin folks are. This comes from projecting self-loathing onto others. Change the pattern by seeing every person as a unique individual, a divine creation even, someone who *has* a body but *is* a soul. Respect every person for what he or she knows and for everything this man or woman has experienced. And enlarge your idea of what is acceptable, attractive, and beautiful in a physical way. You'll have the opportunity to do more of this in Chapter 87, "Visit an Art Museum." For now, aim to see the beauty in yourself and others, when it's obvious and when it isn't.

It wasn't long ago that *beautiful* in this country meant "all-American girl"—Caucasian, of northern European ancestry, under twenty-five. In recent years we have become sufficiently sophisticated as a society to recognize as beauties women of all ethnic backgrounds. And although older women are still not sufficiently appreciated, the Tina Turners of this world are making inroads there. We need to increase our sophistication about body size, too: rounder people, shorter people, all people can be beautiful. We don't need different bodies so much as different eyes.

15

WRITE WHAT YOU EAT AND
KEEP ON WRITING

~

Sometimes we have no idea what we've been eating or how much

until we see it on paper instead of on a plate.

WHEN YOU WRITE DOWN what you eat, you know what's going on. It gives you valuable information. It provides you with clarity. Start today to write what you eat in your journal, your day planner, or a spiral notebook earmarked for the purpose. Some people lose weight doing nothing but this, because it causes them to realize how much cream makes its way into all those cups of coffee, how much dressing is going on those healthy salads, and how many heretofore unnoticed nibbles cross their lips each day. Sometimes we have no idea what we've been eating or how much until we see it on paper instead of on a plate.

Writing your food can open the door to the truth that sets you free. You can record the type and amount of exercise you do, too, if you like. Keeping track of your food and activity levels can grow into full-fledged journal keeping, a practice that can help you know yourself better, access more of your inner wisdom, solve problems more effectively, and deepen your spiritual life. Writing thoughts, feelings, *and* food in a journal can be a true boon to long-term weight loss. It's a way not only to keep track of what you eat but also to provide insights on the connection between what you eat and how you feel. Writing in a journal can be an outlet for uncomfortable feelings that might otherwise lure you down the snack aisle.

If you've never kept a journal—or if the last time was when you were twelve and had a powder-pink diary that locked with a diminutive key—you may want to start with a guided journal, a special book that provides questions to spur your writing. Otherwise just write. Sometimes it will be cathartic, like "Tuesday. I am so mad at my boyfriend I'm about to explode. He just isn't hearing me. It is so frustrating. I feel invisible." Other times it will be healing: "Wednesday. We talked. It's better. He's still not very communicative, but at least he listened, or seemed to. Relationships are so hard, but I can tell he's trying, too. I have to remember that."

There will be days that you'll note your own brilliance: "Thursday. I realized this morning that quality and quantity can be interchangeable. When I have better things, I need fewer of them." And on other days you'll simply record events, describe your dreams (hopes-and-wishes dreams and the ones you have at night), or put prayers on paper. I suspect that God appreciates letters, being so bombarded with auditory requests.

What you write is what you need to write. Write as much as you need and stop when you're finished. Keep your journal in a private place, because it is a private document. Save old journals if you want to read them later and see how far you've come. Or throw each one away when you finish it and move, unencumbered, onto a clean page.

16

Let Your Body Determine
Its Right Size and Shape

~

Whatever your hereditary tendencies, there is an optimal size

and shape for your body. The body itself knows what that is and,

given half a chance, it will get there.

I SAW THIS ON THE INTERNET not long ago: "Click here to find your right summer weight." Summer weight? What are we, motor oil? This latest rendition of the time-honored weight chart reminded me of how curious it is that many of us believe we need to be told what we ought to weigh. Nobody provides this information for wild animals, and they do okay. Why is it so hard for us to believe that we live in bodies capable of determining their appropriate size and shape?

Every human body was designed to function optimally within its own narrow range of shape-size parameters. The body comes with a template of its proper dimensions. These change at certain times—e.g., a woman needs more fat stores when she is pregnant or nursing than at most other times of her life. Still, your body will come into line with that internal template when you treat it well with good food, exercise, and rest, and you don't force it to fit into some unnatural mold.

Your bone structure (small, medium, or large, with wide or narrow hips, wide or narrow shoulders, long or short legs) is yours for life. Your body type, whether it's ectomorphic (delicate), mesomorphic (solid), or endomorphic (curvy), is encoded in your DNA. So is the basic way people in your family are shaped. "Pears" tend to have thin arms and small breasts, thick hips, and heavy thighs. "Apples" are round in the middle—breasts, waist, tummy. Rather than pining over what you'll never be, shoot for becoming the best example of a large-boned, mesomorphic "pear" you can. This is a laudable aim. It shows respect for yourself and acceptance of reality.

Whatever your hereditary tendencies, there is an optimal size and shape for your body. The body itself knows what that is and, given half a chance, it will get there. You do the maintenance— the self-care, the smart choices—and let your body morph into its ideal. This is one ideal you will be able to sustain without herculean effort for the rest of your life.

17

MUCH OF THE TIME, ORDER THE SMALL SIZE

~

Much of the time, small—whether it's actually called small

or some euphemism—is adequate.

A SMALL STEP THAT CAN bear disproportionately hefty dividends is to order the small size much of the time. This is a particularly salient point in reference to foods and beverages that provide minimal nutritional value. The large salad is one thing; the large soda, fries, or cappuccino is something else.

Nowadays you have to go out of your way to get the small size, because marketers find it offensive. Thus "small" has become "large," "tall," or at least "regular." Fountain Cokes used to be six, eight, and ten ounces. Now you can serve yourself a quart or more at any gas station. Back in 1970, McDonald's offered only one size of fries, today's "small," which can seem almost microscopic when compared to medium, large, and "supersize."

When you go to the movies, many theaters will give you free seconds on popcorn—if you order the punch bowl–sized tub to start out with. Fast-food places, coffeehouses, and some chain restaurants give financial incentives for ordering gargantuan portions by making the jumbo drink or the he-man order only slightly costlier than the more reasonable size. (This is if you can even *find* the smaller size: convenience stores routinely place the small cups out of sight and easy reach.)

Don't let these clever businesspeople con you. Much of the time, small—whether it's actually called small or some euphemism—is adequate. When you're in the habit of routinely ordering the small size, it will soon start to seem normal, even ample. And when you choose a larger portion, it's because you really want it. This lets you, not some corporation, choose.

There is nothing wrong with eating or drinking until you've had enough. Chances are, though, you can get full without half a pound of beef and forty ounces of soda. Start with the small size. Eat or drink slowly. Sit with how you feel afterward. Was it enough? If not, do you think you need more of whatever it was, or would something different be more satisfying? Or are you "hungry" for something else entirely: a loving touch, the resolution to a conflict, more recognition for who you are or what you do?

Also, think about—and perhaps do some writing on—the way ordering the small size makes you feel. Does it seem punitive, like being on a diet? Do you feel you're being cheap with yourself? Does the little kid inside you want to whine, "Not the *itty-bitty* one"? If you get these responses, where did they come from? What can you do with them? Who can you talk to who would understand and be able to provide some insights?

Thin people often order the small size. That's part of why they're thin. They don't do it to keep from gaining weight; they do it because they know how much is enough, and often *small* is just right.

18

STAY CENTERED IN TODAY

Forever and next weekend can take care of themselves.

You take care of today.

IT'S DANGEROUS TO GET caught up in "When I get thin . . . ," "When I get this thing licked . . . ," and other states of future glory. This is the day you've got. No matter how praiseworthy your eating and exercise are today, your weight isn't going to be very different when you go to bed tonight from when you got up this morning. The tiny changes will add up, but don't concern yourself too much with them. Just stay in today.

When you do that, you can't stuff yourself and promise that you'll be extra "good" tomorrow, because there is no tomorrow. Today is it, and what you do today is all that matters. Staying centered in the now keeps you aware of what you're doing. You're far less likely to eat absentmindedly when you're firmly rooted in this day, this meal, this project, this conversation. When you stay focused, you fully experience the day—its events, its sensations, its nuances. Life will become richer and more gratifying. You'll have fewer regrets, because regrets belong to the past. You'll worry less, because worry is about the future, and when the future becomes the present it won't be nearly as frightening. The present almost never is.

Think about it: did you ever anguish over trying to lose some set amount of weight for a wedding or a class reunion and not lose as much as you'd wanted, or any at all? If you went to the event anyway, how did it go? Most people would say that, unless they chose to be melodramatically miserable, they had a pretty good time. You usually do when you step into the present, willing to be part of it.

Keeping your focus on the here and now also makes it deliciously possible to eat the way you want to. Trying to do this forever or for a week or some other unwieldy amount of time is asking for trouble. If you convince yourself you can never, ever have one, you'll fantasize over pastries that haven't even been invented yet. Forever and next weekend can take care of themselves. You take care of today. I think that's why the Lord's Prayer says, "Give us this day our daily bread." Why think about more than that? You'd either overeat today or be stuck with stale bread tomorrow.

An added incentive for staying in today is that this is where everything is happening: life, pleasure, accomplishment. Today is an amusement park with all the rides up and running. Don't wait to get your ticket. You're already here.

19

Take the Responsibility, Not the Blame

Blame is demeaning; responsibility is empowering.

You are responsible for dealing with your food choices and your exercise habits, but having a weight problem is not your fault. We live in a culture that is stark raving mad when it comes to food and body size. On the one hand we're heir to a dietary norm replete with fast food, fried food, processed foods, and sugary snacks and beverages. This kind of eating could have given Mahatma Gandhi the physique of a sumo wrestler. Conversely, the media implies that we're all supposed to be skinny. (And women are supposed to be skinny and simultaneously have large breasts—a combination that is, without either having surgery or nursing twins, as rare as the black-footed ferret.)

Do not blame yourself for failing to thrive in this schizophrenic milieu that presents every opportunity to be fat while shaming and belittling you for not being thin. The reason to stop blaming yourself is partly to make you feel better, but mostly it's to get you to take responsibility. If you blame yourself, you can get caught in the cycle of "Oh, I'm such a mess. I just can't do this. What's wrong with me? I may as well stop at the bakery."

If instead of taking the blame you take responsibility, you put yourself on solid ground. In addition to being born into this queer culture, you may have been raised on less than optimal food. You may have experienced childhood traumas that caused you to retreat into Oreos and ice cream, and you're retreating there to this day. You may have gained weight after an illness or following a couple of back-to-back pregnancies. Or it may have crept up on you through years of sitting at a desk on the same floor as the vending machines. Whatever the particulars, you are not to blame, but if you refuse to take responsibility for the state you're in, you'll stay in it—or it will get worse.

Say these two sentences aloud, leaving some silence after each one. First: "I take responsibility for my life." Then: "It's all my fault." How did you feel after making the first statement? How about the second? This exercise alone should convince you to discard blame and accept responsibility at the outset. Blaming yourself—or even speaking words of blame to yourself—makes you weak; being responsible—even if you're just repeating a statement to that effect—makes you strong. Blame keeps you stuck in childhood; responsibility allows you to be an adult. Blame is demeaning; responsibility is empowering.

This change of attitude will play out in your life. Take the simple act of passing on dessert. In a blaming state of mind you might think, "I wish I could have a piece of pie, but I won't because I'm a fat pig and don't deserve anything good." Think that way long enough and you'll eat a whole pie. Straight from the freezer.

Coming from a place of responsibility, you could say no to the pie, or choose fresh fruit instead, with the thought "That was a pleasant dinner. It will feel good to go to bed without being so stuffed that I'd wake up sluggish in the morning." Do you see the difference? In the first example "no pie" is punitive. In the second it's nurturing.

When you take responsibility, you also become more rational. Absurdities like overeating today because you'll diet tomorrow or next Monday show themselves for what they are. The idea that some eating "doesn't count" or that you'll "walk it off" with extra time on the treadmill might come up, but when it does you'll see it as a throwback to the way you used to think, a way that doesn't work anymore.

You are not to blame. If you can't convince yourself of this, accept absolution from me. If I'm not official enough, go to a clergy person and get yourself formally forgiven for the sin of gluttony so you can go out and start fresh. Do whatever it takes for you, given who you are and the way you see the world, to stop blaming yourself so you can start changing yourself.

20

IF YOU HAVE A SERIOUS PROBLEM,
TAKE SERIOUS ACTION

⌒

If you have a history of eating binges, or if you've fasted

to lose weight or vomited to "get rid of" food,

stop reading and contact Overeaters Anonymous.

WOMEN ALMOST ALWAYS want to lose weight. Sometimes they need to for health reasons, to feel better, or to live better. Other times our thin-obsessed culture has convinced them that utopia is simply a ten-pound loss away.

There are, however, other women—and men—who are eating themselves to death. That could be a literal death from anorexia, bulimia, or complications of obesity. More likely it's a living death of self-deprecation and despair.

If you've dieted numerous times, joined weight loss clubs, and gone to doctors to help you eat less, stop reading this book. If you have a shelf filled with diet books and clothing in as many sizes as Macy's carries, stop reading. If you have a history of eating binges, or if you've fasted to lose weight or vomited to "get rid of " food, stop reading and contact Overeaters Anonymous. You can write or E-mail them (addresses are in the "Resources and Recommended Reading" section at the end of this book). Better yet, look up Overeaters Anonymous in your local white pages. Call the number. Get to the first meeting you can, even if it's half an hour from now.

Get to as many meetings as possible. Learn all you can and put what you learn into practice. Get people's phone numbers and call somebody every day. The only exception to all this is if you wander into a meeting where someone is pushing a diet, any diet. These are offshoot meetings that aren't giving you pure, diet-free recovery. Walk out. Find a different meeting.

Real OA is, as its own literature states, "not a diet and calories club." Like Alcoholics Anonymous, on which it was founded, it is a spiritual program. This has nothing to do with religion; it is spiritual because it deals with inner change. Nothing short of profound inner change will save your life if you are indeed an addictive eater. I offer this suggestion even if you have gone to OA before and it didn't work, or you didn't like it, or you didn't like somebody there. Try it again. There are other ways for compulsive overeaters to recover, but this is the most reliable way I know of. It is time tested, supported by free-will donations (you pay as much as you can, even if that's nothing), and everybody is welcome.

You can still read this book. You will, in fact, get a great deal out of it. If you are a compulsive eater, however, you will not be able to apply its counsel consistently without help. It's like this. Let's say that, instead of this suggestion and the others you're reading, my experience had convinced me that the way to permanent weight loss was to get up and walk across the room. If you were just somebody wanting to lose weight, I could say, "Walk across the room." Since you would be perfectly capable of doing that, you would either do it and reap the benefits or opt not to for some reason of your own—distrust of me, the desire to try something else first, whatever.

If you're a compulsive eater, though, you would be like someone with two broken legs. I could say, "Walk across the room," and you might be eager to do it. You might want to walk across the room with all that's in you. Nevertheless, because of your two broken legs, a significant amount of healing would have to take place before you could accomplish what someone else could do with hardly a thought to the matter.

If you believe that you have two broken legs as far as eating and weight are concerned, go to OA meetings. Call the people you meet there. Get help. Get well. Reading this book can be part of your process, just not all of it.

EAT ENOUGH

⁓

Since you feed your goldfish and your hamster and your Great

Dane enough food for a goldfish, a hamster, and a Great Dane,

you need to feed your precious human self enough for you.

WHO THINKS ABOUT MONEY all the time? People who are broke. And who thinks about food all the time? People who are hungry. Instead, eat enough. If you don't trust your own appetite shutoff mechanism, watch the people around you who eat sanely. They may seem to eat more at meals than you do, but chances are they're eating lighter fare and they don't eat between meals; there are more pressing things to do. Have as your goal learning to eat moderately, not marginally. There is a difference.

This may seem to contradict the earlier suggestion about ordering the small size. It doesn't. For starters, the small size may well be enough. And with nutritionally questionable foods, small is plenty. Here we're talking about the food that keeps you alive and well. You need enough of it. Skimping taken to the extreme is anorexia; the less severe version is obsessive dieting that, even when it doesn't endanger physical health, is an awful way to live.

I have a theory that a lot of us periodically undereat because we believe it is somehow virtuous. Saying "I went all day without eating" will get you comments like "Gosh, how do you do that?" and "I wish I had that much willpower." In truth, without extenuating circumstances—such as fasting as a religious observance or because you don't feel well—going all day without food is not a balanced thing to do. We're impressed by it, I think, because a lot of us are unconsciously embarrassed that we're humans and not angels. We have to eat and do laundry and fix things that break—stuff that angels can fly right by. Because we're uncomfortable about the earthier aspects of the human condition, we admire people who don't eat much (or don't seem to), who don't sleep much (they may have insomnia), or who don't show emotion (they may wish they could).

Eat! It's good for you. Listen well: I am not saying "Eat yourself sick" or "Eat to deal with your emotions." I am not saying "Eat because you're bored and there's nothing better to do" or "Eat and hate yourself and then either throw up or run five miles." I am simply suggesting that, since you feed your goldfish and your hamster and your Great Dane enough food for a goldfish, a hamster, and a Great Dane, you need to feed your precious human self enough for you. Some days you'll eat a little more, some days you'll eat a little less, but every day you can feel safe and be proud of yourself.

WEAR CLOTHES YOU LIKE IN YOUR CURRENT SIZE

A surefire way to feel fat, regardless of how much you weigh,

is to wear clothes that are too tight, that are too bulky,

or that you just don't like much.

CLOTHES MAY NOT MAKE the man (or woman), but they can make the attitude. Ralph Waldo Emerson wrote, "The sense of being perfectly well-dressed gives a feeling of inward tranquillity which religion is powerless to bestow." I'm sure that was a bit of nineteenth-century tongue-in-cheek, but he had a point. When your clothes reinforce, rather than contradict, your personality, you feel more confident and you have a better day.

A surefire way to feel fat, regardless of how much you weigh, is to wear clothes that are too tight, that are too bulky, or that you just don't like. We all acquire some of these from time to time, but learning to shop astutely and bravely discard past mistakes is more important than it might sound.

Part of feeling good about yourself in the here and now is to dress becomingly in clothes that fit your current contours, colors that lift your spirits, and styles that appeal to your aesthetic sense. Clothes like this are made in every size. Even though many high-profile designers conceive of garments more suited to the runway than to real bodies in the real world, there are plenty of clothes out there. Find a few that you love.

Refuse to let fashion victimize you by believing that you are faulty and need to apologize for wearing the size you do. If the store where you're shopping doesn't offer a selection for you, it's the store's fault, not yours. It's missing out on the opportunity to have your business and that of a lot of other people with cash in their wallets. Go somewhere else.

Waiting until you've lost weight to enjoy fashion or buy something new is also a sign of victim mentality. In that frame of mind we could all convince ourselves that we're too short, too old, too flat-chested, too pregnant, too undeserving, or too something else to go shopping and buy ourselves something we'll enjoy. If you're breathing, you deserve this much.

When you shop for clothing, look for good design. Good fabrics. Good workmanship—the best you can afford. The clothes you take home should be comfortable, becoming, and speak to you in some way. "Okay, this will do" isn't good enough.

Use clothing to express yourself. Women who have been full-figured for a long time often come to a sense of their personal style and put together fabulous wardrobes. Yo-yo dieters who were a size four last year and a fourteen now have the most trouble. They feel that if they can't wear what they used to, they'd just as soon ignore the whole business until they're thin again. This is a self-defeating move. If you're looking to be fit from within, you're willing to take a holistic view in which your life—every irreplaceable day of it—matters more than your size.

If you have only a few pieces in your closet that make you feel terrific every time you put them on, wear these the most and add to your wardrobe as soon as you can. Yes, I know you're losing weight and whatever you buy won't fit for long. Don't worry about it. When it doesn't fit anymore, you can get it altered or take it to a consignment shop. What matters is that you look and feel presentable today. You can worry about tomorrow when it shows up.

HAVE SOME BREAKFAST

Experiment with what morning foods and

amounts of food feel right to you, give you energy,

and sustain you until lunchtime.

HAVE SOME BREAKFAST. This is different from "Eat a big breakfast." Not everyone is cut out for eating a lot in the morning. These people are better off with something light—fruit or cereal. Others of us do better with a full A.M. meal. You knew which type of person you were by the time you were ten. Respect that. Just eat something for breakfast so you're not going out into the world with your blood sugar lagging, making every doughnut shop and fast-food billboard a grave temptation. Experiment with what morning foods and amounts of food feel right to you, give you energy, and sustain you until lunchtime.

In the summer I like smoothies in the morning—bananas, frozen strawberries, soy milk, and a nutrient powder with protein and vitamins in it. When it's cold, I prefer hot cereal with sliced fruit and slivered almonds and flaxseed oil. Sometimes I go to one of my favorite coffeehouses in the morning (I like to write there—no phones, clerical tasks, or household chores interfering) and have a chai latté and a cranberry scone. That's me. You may like breakfasts of an entirely different sort. No problem there. Just eat something in the morning: something that tastes good to you and that makes you feel that you've done yourself a favor.

Lighten Up

~

Impress upon yourself this eternal truth: Most things

don't amount to a hill of beans.

LIGHTEN UP IS A LOVELY metaphor: when you can do it with your attitude, your body is apt to follow. Of course some things are serious. That doesn't mean we have to take everything seriously, especially not ourselves. If someone cuts in front of you in line, you are not obligated to make a moral issue out of it. If there is toilet paper stuck to your shoe, you don't have to be mortified. Try amused instead. If you have a different opinion from someone else, it is probably not imperative that this person *understand* your point of view, and explaining it for the fifteenth time will not clarify your position any better than the first fourteen explanations did.

Impress upon yourself this eternal truth: Most things don't amount to a hill of beans. In the majority of endeavors winning is overrated, and in most human interactions one-upping is far less pleasant than two conversing. The arguments, jealousies, and misunderstandings that can make life so unpleasant—and send many an overeater to the nearest microwave—are, for the most part, insignificant. Let them go or "let go and let God."

You don't have to appear brilliant, sophisticated, and on top of things every minute of your life. It's okay to hear the name of a writer or politician or composer and say, "Who's that?" Sincerity is far more appealing than pretense. "I don't know" is a legitimate answer to a host of questions, and "I'm not going to worry about this now" is a legitimate response to a host of troubles. Refusing to fret over what you can do nothing about is closely related to refusing to eat over what you can do nothing about. Do your best to be less distraught when things don't work out the way you'd hoped they would. More often than not, this means that life has something better in store for you anyhow.

GET UP, GET DRESSED, GET GOING

Lethargy and isolation are overeating's best friends;

mobility is its archenemy.

EARLY IN MY PROCESS of losing weight for the last time, I remember being sad and afraid. I wanted to stay home, preferably in bed, and not have to deal with everything. That's when it came to me: "Get up, get dressed, get going." It became my mantra for those early months. Remember Newton's Law about a body in motion staying in motion and one that's at rest staying that way? It applies here. Lethargy and isolation are overeating's best friends; mobility is its archenemy.

After I'd been working with this idea for a while—getting up and getting out, even when it felt as overwhelming as playing catch with Atlas—I came upon a line in a poem by Milton that read, "Awake, arise, or forever be fallen." I took this as an affirmation that I was on the right track. Take this tip for yourself: get up, get dressed, get going—or adapt the sentiment more poetically if you'd like. However you phrase it, the fact remains that when you are doing other things you aren't doing inappropriate eating. When your body is occupied, your mind is, too. So—get up, get dressed, get going. You'll probably even have a good time.

I had to use this technique years later, during a rough period that took up an entire season: the winter of my discontent, to borrow a phrase. My daughter and I were in New York. We both got some killer flu and were down for over a month, unable to help each other and barely capable of walking the dog. The sun didn't shine from January till April. At least that's how I remember it. To escape the weather, a mouse moved into our apartment. And brought his family. And his nation.

At first I just felt sorry for myself and complained a lot. Complaining can be good; it gets things off your chest. You have to learn to complain constructively, though. Constructive complaining is based on passing it around. If you complain to the same one or two people over and over, you'll develop a relationship dynamic based on your whining and their consoling—for as long as they'll do it, of course. After a while they get tired of listening and you're on your own.

When I knew I was close to having complained to as many people as I could and still have friends, I took more assertive action. I hired a dog walker, demanded rodent proofing, and as soon as I was well enough, I knew it was time to get up, get dressed, and get going. I took a trip home to Kansas City, spending time with people who still liked me since I hadn't complained to them too much. They helped me psych myself up for going back and giving winter in the big city one more shot.

When I returned to New York, I made myself get up, get dressed, and get going every day. I forced myself to have fun even when fun was too cold and too inconvenient. I stood in line in drizzly rain to get half-price theater tickets. I went to yoga class and was tempted to ask the people on either side of me, "Was it easy for you to get here, or did you have to push yourself, too?" I invited friends and colleagues to meet me for lunches, and for the most part they said yes. By the time spring showed up in earnest, I was getting invitations, too.

When you get up, get dressed, and get going, you inform the universe that you're here, you're ready, and you intend to get in the game. You don't have to feel like it. You just have to do it.

26

SEE YOURSELF RIGHT

Being humble isn't putting yourself down but seeing yourself

without judgments, whether they're weighted toward

canonization or infamy.

YOU CAN SPEND A LOT of energy trying to become the right size when it may be more valuable to be in the right place—that is, to see yourself clearly for who and what you are. You know about seeing yourself accurately in the physical sense and how someone suffering from anorexia can look at her emaciated reflection and see a fat person looking back. Seeing yourself right goes beyond the physical, though: it's having a true picture of who you are as an individual and in relation to those around you.

When I was eating to get through life instead of just to stay in it, I sometimes considered myself worthless, barely deserving the air I breathed and the space I occupied. But I could also feel superior, like I knew more or had more talents than other people. Both extremes were not only wrong but damaging, and I couldn't get past them until I learned a little something about humility.

Believe me, I did this under duress. I figured any word that had the same root as *humiliation* wasn't one I wanted anything to do with. But I did learn about humility, because I couldn't get to know myself any other way, and without coming to know myself I'd have kept communing with éclairs. When I looked at humility with a somewhat open mind, I came to understand that being humble isn't putting yourself down but seeing yourself without judgments, whether they're weighted toward canonization or infamy.

Like everybody else, you and I have every right to our share of the best of everything. If we weren't magnificent, we wouldn't be here. And if we were perfect, we wouldn't be here either.

27

Make Peace with Your Past and Other People

~

The past may be over, but it's not necessarily done with.

W HEN A GRAIN OF SAND irritates an oyster, a pearl results. When a nagging memory irritates a practicing overeater, a binge results. The past may be over, but it's not necessarily done with. Until it is, it can lead to a return to unproductive eating. Wading in old hurts and disappointments is hardly a day at the beach, but without being willing to face the deep-seated issues that may be responsible for at least some of your food problem, you may never solve it.

An effective way to make peace is to forgive the people who harmed you and forgive yourself for your own mistakes. You deal with the instances in which you were at fault by showing up, 'fessing up, and setting things right to the degree that you can. Then you have to let it go. If letting go is hard for you, keep at it. It's hard for nearly everybody, but it's a required course.

When someone has hurt you, forgiveness can be a slippery slope. On the one hand, you don't want to become a doormat and give anyone the impression that treating you badly is acceptable. This is particularly true if you were abused as a child or by a partner who was supposed to love you. On the other hand, forgiveness is not saying, "It's okay that you were terrible to me. You can do it again anytime." It is, rather, realizing that hurt comes from hurt and, knowing that, releasing the person who harmed you to his or her own fate. This is as much for you as it is for the other person. You need the weight of what happened lifted from your shoulders and your soul.

To go more deeply into making peace with your past, you may need to employ a therapist you can trust and relate to. If you don't feel comfortable with the first one you see, consult someone else. This isn't like trying a new hairstylist and figuring that any mistakes will grow back. A therapist is somebody you're allowing into your psyche. Be choosy—at least as choosy as your HMO will let you be. A well-trained, empathetic professional can be a godsend in helping you maneuver through the maze of past events. You may pride yourself on self-reliance, but if some of the experiences that shaped your life, and perhaps contributed to the way you use food, took place when you were a small child, it is unlikely that you can work through these on your own.

You'd hire a guide if you were going to a foreign land where you didn't speak the language. The human mind is like a country that is still not fully explored. It has a language of its own, and a good therapist can translate. She can't keep food out of your mouth, but she can be unsurpassed in helping you realize why you put it there. She may also guide you to a series of "Aha!" moments so that things that never made sense before can start coming clear.

If you've had therapy or counseling in the past and found it wanting, you may have been with the wrong therapist, or it may have been the wrong time. I went to several counselors before I stopped eating myself silly and was disappointed in every one of them. I realize now that I was expecting more from them than they could give. I wanted a miracle. That's not too much to ask—miracles happen all the time—but it is too much to ask of another human being, regardless of the credentials on her office wall. Let a therapist help you work through the past. Let a Higher Power transform your future.

28

LET OTHER PEOPLE
DO IT THEIR WAY

What other people do is irrelevant.

GET USED TO IT: other people are trying to lose weight, too, and they're going to do it their way. The vast majority of them will fail, but regardless of how well or how poorly they fare, let them do it their way. You stay with the path you're on.

People go into raptures about their diets more than about religion, politics, or the relative superiority of their own children. These dieters have seen the light, this week at least, and they want you to see it, too. If this beatific vision involves selling you something multilevel, it's even worse. Say, "Thank you very much. I'm doing something myself that is working well for me." Don't offer details; it will just get you into a discussion that neither of you needs.

It's no easy task to change from a self-centered to a spirit-centered way of being, get to know yourself from the inside out, and restructure the various habit patterns that will result in a fit body for the rest of your life. Hearing that someone you know lost thirty pounds doing this thing or that can turn your head. The promise of "quick and easy" would tempt a saint. Hold firm to your resolve. You're changing your life, not just your pants size.

Right now someone you know is probably eating nothing but slabs of rare meat. Another is drinking meal-replacement drinks and eating meal-replacement bars. Someone else is fasting. Another person is working out two hours a day, four on weekends. Somebody is counting calories, somebody else fat grams, and a third is calculating "points" on some plan or another.

Let them cipher to their hearts' content. Wish them well. For your part, strive to put food in perspective in your life— somewhere beneath God, country, family, work, good deeds, good sex, good times, and making your mark on the world. What other people do is irrelevant.

29

GIVE THANKS
BEFORE AND AFTER MEALS

It is just about impossible to say grace over a binge.

RELIGIOUS PEOPLE ARE familiar with saying grace before meals, a practice that anyone who wants to eat reasonably and has a record of doing otherwise may wish to adopt. Obviously, if you don't believe in the traditional God, you won't say a traditional grace. You might not *say* anything, just pause. Center yourself. Be grateful that you have food to eat and that you're willing to sit here for a moment without scarfing it all down as if there will never be any more.

Moments of quiet, moments of thanks, moments of remembering that there's more to life than just getting by are precious whenever you can get them. For a variety of reasons they are especially useful as you sit down to a meal. First, it is just about impossible to say grace over a binge. It's ludicrous to think of sitting in your car with bags of sweet and salty stuff that you intend to inhale in short order and say, "Bless us, oh Lord, in these thy gifts which we are about to receive . . . " or any other mealtime prayer. I challenge you to try to do it. I wouldn't be surprised if some people could lose weight and keep it off for life by doing nothing other than eating only what they can, in good conscience, ask a blessing on.

Then there is the calmness factor. Since a lot of overeating is done to take the edge off, even sedate us to a degree, coming to meals with a tranquil mind makes a lot of sense. We can't get a massage, do a half-hour meditation, or have a session with a life coach before every meal, but taking even one minute to get quiet, breathe deeply, and think some thankful thoughts or say some thankful words can put us in a calm frame of mind, too. When we are, we're likely to eat sensibly, enjoy the experience, digest the food well, and not have that nagging desire for something more or something different.

In addition, there is the notion of a *blessing* itself. Every religion and culture has some version of the blessing, of consecrating something physical, whether a meal or a marriage, and thereby giving it divine sanction. Whether anything actually happens when a blessing is invoked is a question of faith, but science has looked at faith in recent years, and some of its findings are fascinating. One study had Eastern holy men pick out from an array of dishes the ones that had had grace said over them. They were able to do it. Whether this means that food graced by a grace carries a benediction for those who consume it, I can't say. I only know that if I have a choice, I'd rather eat blessed food than the other kind.

For people who have had trouble with food, saying thank you *after* meals may be even more valuable than saying thank you before them. After all, people with food issues don't have any trouble sitting down to a meal; it's getting up that can be tough.

I shared this story in my book *Love Yourself Thin*, but it bears repeating: Someone I know who was working to overcome an overeating pattern accompanied a Roman Catholic acquaintance to Mass. At the close of the service, the priest said, "The Mass is ended. Go in peace." My friend adapted those words as an after-eating prayer: "The meal is ended. I go in peace." It helped her, and her telling me about it helped me. You may want to use it, too, or something similar. Any simple, even silent, after-meal thank-you can be the mental punctuation that tells you the meal is over and life awaits.

30

CARE LESS

Lose the desperation, lose the weight.

IF LOSING WEIGHT is of utmost importance to you, care less. While eating sanely and developing your inner life need to be high-priority items, fixating on weight is problematic. I know you can't force yourself to stop wanting a trim body, nor should you, but you can care about it a little less. The reason is that what we focus on gets bigger, more problematic. It's like watched pots that refuse to boil.

Look at the way this principle has worked in other areas. Were you ever obsessed with having a relationship and couldn't seem to get a date? Did you finally give it up, focus on other things, and all of a sudden become Ms. or Mr. Popularity? It happens all the time. I don't know why relationship counselors aren't telling their single clients, "Buy property." Almost every single person I know who stopped waiting for romance to show up and bought himself or herself a house or a condo has ended up partnered within a short time. In buying their own homes, they made a bold statement to the universe: "I am getting along just fine, thank you." That strength and stability is attractive.

When you want something too desperately, whether it's a lover, a promotion, or to fit into last year's jeans, that desperation can keep what you want at bay. In the fit-from-within context: lose the desperation, lose the weight.

The easiest way to care less about how much you weigh, how much you lose, and how much you get to eat while you're losing it is to care more about something else. This can be a hobby, a cause, creative work—anything that you can be passionate about and that you can count on to be there. It should not depend on another person. Developing a romantic infatuation, for instance, is a great way to lose weight in the short run, but the weight is destined to return if the relationship doesn't work out (or even if it does work out but Prince or Princess Charming is found to be a mere mortal after all).

You can also come to care less about focusing on your body by developing a wide range of interests. I think of this as becoming a "life gourmet." I love being around people like this. They have fascinating information about all sorts of topics, and if you ask them if they'd like to go to the opera or the bowling alley, they'll likely say yes and have a great time. You become a life gourmet by expanding the parameters of what's comfortable for you. A lot of us keep magnificent experiences out of our experience because we've fenced ourselves in with our own fears and prejudices:

Cruise to Alaska? "Too cold. And I might get seasick."

White-water rafting? "Too much sun. And I might get riversick."

Dinner at a Turkish restaurant? "I don't speak the language. And my stomach is sensitive, you know."

Parade, fireworks, theater in the park? "Mosquitoes are just crazy about me, and in a crowd like that it's hard to see anything."

Thrift-store shopping? "You don't really know who's worn those clothes, and I get allergies in musty places."

This is an exaggeration (I hope), but you get the idea. The old ways are comfortable. Dependable. You can count on a candy bar to be like every other candy bar. The sitcom will almost always come on at its right time, its right night, and with its reliable laugh track. Expanding yourself, on the other hand, can feel awkward. Give it time. Care less. Your goal is to put food and weight in their proper perspective. You can do this by enriching your life and caring about that.

31

Don't Let the Details Get You Down

~

Minutia is fattening.

MINUTIA IS FATTENING. It can bog you down in an apparently endless spiral of errands, chores, deadlines, and details that are not pivotal in creating the life you want but that seem inescapable in the life you've got. Recreational eating is an agreeable diversion when the details get you down. When you're in the midst of a double-fudge anything, it doesn't matter that you have a paper to write, the lawn guy didn't show up, and if you don't do laundry soon, you'll have to pick up spare underwear in a three-pack at the drugstore. Of course, when the only fudge left is on your upper lip, the paper is still due, the grass is still growing, and the laundry hasn't gone anywhere.

Face it: boring details are part of life. When you are truly present while you do them, and if you take them one at a time, they're not so bad. A commitment to doing them honorably and well reshapes them as spiritual practice. And without them, what would we compare the thrilling stuff to? Still, we don't need so many boring details that life becomes a grind. Most of us don't realize that although some of the tedium in our lives comes with the privilege of being human, a great deal of it we generate for ourselves.

Being involved with details shields us from having to get involved with the important things. The reason many people have so much trouble managing their time is that those Cs on their ABC to-do lists (A—vital; B—necessary; C—trivial) can be the most enticing tasks on the list. Why? Because it takes minimal effort to file those invoices, make a grocery list, and buy stamps from the machine at the post office. (That's actually fun: they give you your change in those interesting dollar coins.) This is not to say that the filing, the marketing, and the mailing don't need to get done, but if you fill your life with activities like these, the things you really want to do don't have a prayer. And that's worth eating over.

I often hear people say something along the lines of "I would get my master's [or travel abroad, become a foster parent, write a musical, have you over for dinner], but you know, it's just so time-consuming to take care of an old house." If this person *loves* taking care of the old house, brims with delight every time she gets to work on the plumbing, and has never once said, "I'll get to those baseboards as soon as I eat the rest of the nachos," maintenance of a vintage home is not a boring detail for her. If, on the other hand, she is single-handedly supporting the corn chip people because she resents having to keep up this monstrosity, the details have her down.

Do a minutia assessment of your own days and evenings. How much time do you spend, either at your job or after hours, performing tasks that offer little reward? Do you find yourself doing the little things first because the big ones are daunting? Which of the details that populate your professional and personal life could you do without, do less, or delegate? This is key, because too many details will weigh you down. That's the last thing you want when you really long to fly.

32

LEARN WHERE YOU STAND
WITH SUGAR

~

Many self-confessed sugar addicts believe that sugar is

for them what alcohol is to an alcoholic. Their safest

stance is to stay away from it.

FOR SOME PEOPLE, eating sugary foods apparently triggers an insatiable craving for more of the same. A "normal" person might eat something very sweet and fatty like a piece of fudge and say, "One is enough for me: this is so rich." People with sugar addictions can hardly understand what *rich* means. For them it's more like "One is too many, and a thousand aren't enough," as the saying goes.

When I say "sugar addiction," don't hold me to the clinical definition of *addiction*. Refined sugar has never been officially classified as an addictive substance. People who have a problem with it, however, say it might as well be heroin. They can have an awful time getting off it, but at least that is possible. Trying to eat it moderately, for many of them, seems not to be.

Also, the sugar problems referred to in this chapter are problems with eating—and having trouble not eating—sweet foods. Sugar metabolism disorders like diabetes and hypoglycemia are something else again. These are medical conditions that require medical care.

All that said, you need to find out how sugar affects you. You can ascertain this for yourself by eating all foods, sweets included, in moderation and seeing how you do. If it works for an extended period, terrific. If, however, you find yourself dogged by cravings for more sugar every time you have a pastry or other sweet, you're better off sticking with fresh fruit for dessert. If this sounds like life at San Quentin with no possibility of parole, you are very likely a sugar addict. Other people just don't care that much.

I know people who believe that eating sugary foods not only sets up an unquenchable desire for more but also affects them mentally. They talk about being in a "sugar fog," unable to think clearly. Some say that being "high on sugar" makes them anxious and argumentative. Others find that they are (appropriately) "sweet" while the sugar is in their system, but they become irritable a few hours after eating it. That's reason enough to reach for some more.

Refined sugar products are the primary culprit, but those sweetened with honey, fructose, molasses, maple syrup, and even fruit juice can be problematic for some people. Sugar/fat combinations—cookies, ice cream, chocolates—seem to be more addictive than sugar on its own—hard candy, sorbet, Jell-O. Dried fruits—raisins, dates, figs, etc.—are exceedingly sweet. Even though its sugar is natural, people with an addictive relationship to sugar can have a hard time with dried fruit, too.

Many self-confessed sugar addicts believe that sugar—and, for some, refined white flour, as well—is for them what alcohol is to an alcoholic. Their safest stance is to stay away from it. Although sweets were among my favorite binge items for years, I do not have an addictive relationship with sugar today. I eat some of it sometimes, but enough is enough. I don't go crazy over it or dream about it afterward. If I did, I'd stop altogether, and my life would not be the least bit diminished because of it.

Get to know yourself so you can protect yourself and care for yourself the way you deserve to be cared for and protected. If you're better off not eating sugar (or anything else that is an indisputable binge trigger for you), staying away from it isn't a punishment. It's a gift.

33

IF YOU EAT DESSERT, SHARE IT

Dessert is for pleasure more than nourishment.

And pleasure is best when it's shared.

WE JUST DISCUSSED SUGAR addiction. Some people simply cannot handle the stuff. For that matter, it's not a good idea for anybody to eat much of it: sugar in excess can depress the immune system, and the blood sugar fluctuations it causes can lead to appetite and mood swings. Still, humans like the sweet taste, and dessert is considered a "treat," something chronic dieters have long denied themselves or labeled *bad* and eaten with guilt and remorse. Instead, if you've honestly looked at your own reaction to sugar and found that you don't respond to it with a nagging craving for more, one way to enjoy both dessert and camaraderie is to share the sweet course.

If you're on a date, it's romantic. If you're with a friend, you can split the cost of the tiramisu and save a little money. Either way, sharing dessert gives you that little something sweet that is sometimes nice at the end of a meal, and it gets you used to the notion of a *little* something sweet—not some whopping portion with a whole day's worth of calories and saturated fat.

I personally did not eat desserts at all for several years. I was afraid to. But the fear dissipated over time. I see now that it lessened in direct proportion to my dedication to forgo eating for a fix. The more committed I became to eating with prudence, the more I was able to do that, and the more leeway I had with my food choices. It doesn't work this way for everyone; that's why exacting honesty is so essential. For myself today, I eat dessert sometimes. I actually prefer to split it. Dessert is for pleasure more than nourishment, and pleasure is best when it's shared.

34

ALTER YOUR DEFINITION OF SUCCESS

Success is not down the road. It can be precisely where you are on the road, right now, today.

FOR WEIGHT LOSS TO LAST, you need to move away from the commonly accepted definition of success in this arena, which is a number on a scale. Instead, start to interpret success as every day you pay attention to your inner life, eat reasonably, and treat yourself and others well. If you get some exercise, give a nod to your creative side, or enjoy yourself a bit more than usual, you get extra credit. Success is not down the road. It can be precisely where you are on the road, right now, today.

Traditionally, people with weight to lose have been goal oriented. That's legitimate when you're out to reach a sales quota, save for a major purchase, or hit the bull's-eye during archery practice, but releasing weight—a preferable term to *losing*, I think—is different. It is not a goal in itself but rather the result of changing your attitude and the way you do things. Therefore, the truest indication that you're winning this battle comes in how you spend your days.

Ask yourself these questions:

- What does my life look like?

- What am I doing with my time?

- How am I treating myself?

- How am I getting along with people?

- What am I eating, and what's going on in my head before, during, and after?

- And—this is the big one—am I scared to death?

Early on, having some fear is normal, especially if you've tried to lose weight many times and found yourself in worse shape after the venture than before. Sometimes this fear comes out in dreams. Don't be surprised if you wake up some night with the awful memory that you just raided the refrigerator or the entire city of Hershey, Pennsylvania. It's okay. People who dream about having eating sprees aren't having them in real life.

When you're getting started, don't be afraid of being afraid. A bit of trepidation might even be a good thing—the way stage fright can lead to a better performance. If it goes on too long, or if you're so afraid that it's interfering with the process of living, confide in someone who knows what you're talking about. Write out your fears in your journal. Get closer to your Higher Power through meditation, prayer, or more time spent in nature.

The idea is to start living fully—and being a success in your own eyes—sooner rather than later. You're succeeding day by day. Remember that. You are entering a bright new world where you will find more opportunities for fulfillment and joy. Expect some of these to come because you've changed the size of your body. Expect more of them because you're changing the state of your heart.

35

Do Whatever It Takes

~

Cravings stop going where they aren't fed.

In the beginning especially, and for as long as necessary, do whatever it takes to keep excess food out of your mouth. In other words, avoid temptation until it is no longer tempting. Maybe this means not having sweets in the house. "But what about my husband and the kids?" Haven't you sacrificed for them once or twice? Give them a turn. They don't need all that sugar either, and heaven knows the world outside is full of the stuff.

If you're out, you're full, and you're still picking at your plate (where is the bus person anyway?), pour enough salt or pepper on what's left that you'll stop. If you buy a box of something that sings to you in the night and you know you're going to eat the whole thing, toss it in the compost bin, annihilate it in the garbage disposal, or flush it down the toilet. Do whatever you need to do. The last time I had to go on a flush-and-destroy mission was about six years ago. I was a dozen years past my last binge, and food was not a problem in my life. I'd bought these little bear-shaped graham crackers for my daughter. She didn't like them, but after I'd had a few they stayed on my mind like a new beau who hadn't called back yet. My serenity was worth more than stupid little bear cookies. I flushed them.

I feel so neutral about food today that it seems as if that could never be necessary again, but it might. And if it happens, to the sewers with it! I spent enough time in the ugly tangle of recrimination, remorse, and indigestion. Feeling good inside and out is a whole lot better.

Therefore, do whatever you have to to keep from eating anything you have that nagging feeling about. You know what feeling I mean. It's that little nudge from your inner self that says, oh so quietly, "If you eat that, you'll feel really rotten," or "I know you're telling yourself you'll have just one, but you know as well as I do that once you start, that box is a goner."

Whatever this food, it has no business passing your lips, not now anyway. It might be some nearly pornographic junk food that you almost never touch, or it might be some perfectly legitimate item that *this time* you know you're not yearning for because you're hungry or because it's what's for dinner, but because you want to eat it for a fix. That's eating to alter your mood, assuage uncomfortable feelings, mitigate anger, dull pain, or deprive yourself of happiness you feel you don't deserve.

When this kind of craving surfaces, take whatever action is called for. Phone a friend who won't make light of your situation. Or get out of yourself: call someone you know has been having a difficult time and ask how you can help. You might play music as loud as the neighbors will let you: the auditory stimulation can jolt you back to clearer thinking. Or take a bath. Answer all 115 of your E-mails. Visit somebody. Retreat to a movie theater or rent yourself a double feature. Hang out in a bookstore. Go to a church and light a candle. Go home and go to bed.

These measures, and others you'll think of, can help you ride out a craving. When you don't give into it, a craving is a short-lived entity. Even the ones that seem as powerful as a tropical storm will fizzle if you occupy yourself some other way. Early on, cravings may crop up quite a bit. One might surprise you occasionally in the future, too, even when people look at you and say, "You could never have been fat." But generally speaking, cravings stop going where they aren't fed. Ride them out often enough and they'll get the message that it's no use bothering you.

36

GET DOWN AND DIRTY WITH LIFE

Food can be delicious, but life can be miraculous.

EATING IS SENSUAL, almost sensuous. Many people who get an inordinate amount of pleasure out of food aren't getting nearly enough from life's other offerings. To this end, get down and dirty with the myriad pleasures proffered you during your time on earth.

Sometimes it's simply a matter of taking the time—and the risk—to experience something sweet at the moment it's in front of you. A while back I was on my way from my house in Kansas City to speak for a writer's conference at a college in the suburbs. It was spring, and I was wearing pale pink. I thought I looked pretty good. I'd driven a mere half-block when I spotted my Rastafarian neighbor out with someone adorable: a roly-poly puppy, stumbling over herself in a way that was totally endearing. I could have driven on in my tidy pink suit to give a tidily prepared talk, but this was too good to miss.

So I parked my car and crossed the street. "Hey, man," my Rastafarian neighbor said. "A lot of people slow down to look at her, but you're the first one who's stopped." He went on to tell me that his new pet was named White Buffalo, and that she was a rare, pure white beagle, just five weeks old. I had never seen such perfect puppyness: the blue eyes, the oversized paws, and great, flapping ears slapping her droopy cheeks as she rolled in the dirt.

I so wanted to pick her up, but I was wearing pale pink. I was to give the keynote address for three hundred eager writers and writers-to-be. If I picked up White Buffalo in all her muddy, dusty glory, I might look like a slob instead of an expert. But if I didn't pick her up, I would be a fraud: someone getting paid to speak about life experience and overcoming and creating from the core of your being, when I wasn't even willing to get my suit messy. So I reached down and scooped up this wriggling, licking, chubby ball of magnificence. It was a blissful experience. And I can bring that feeling back any day that feels devoid of delight.

Yes, she got my pink suit mussed. So what?

I saw White Buffalo only one other time. She was still cute, but she was at that awkward stage of pre-dogdom that wasn't as magical as when she'd had blue eyes and more skin than her bones could accommodate. My Rastafarian neighbor moved shortly after that and took White Buffalo with him. If I had not been willing to give a talk in a less than pristine suit, I would have missed something irreplaceable.

If you want to stay thin and free and balanced—and even happy much of the time—you have to get down in the dirt and pick up the puppy, or do whatever would bring you this kind of bliss. It does not exist in a bag of chips, and Baskin-Robbins has yet to come up with the flavor. Food can be delicious, but life can be miraculous. Get down and dirty with it every chance you get.

37

Join a Friendly Gym

Shop for a gym almost as carefully as you'd shop for a spouse.

In either case, the wrong one will make you miserable.

You can be fit, trim, and healthy without belonging to a gym, but because so many of us have sedentary jobs and sedentary hobbies, belonging to a gym or a health club can make it easier. This is especially true if you want to include weight training in your fitness regimen. It's not for everybody, but resistance exercise does increase muscle mass, and muscle burns fat just for the heck of it. Because weight lifting requires a different kind of stamina from aerobic exercise, being overweight is not an impediment to progress. Physical strength is also a metaphor for inner strength. One can support the other.

Whether you want to join a health club for its weight equipment, swimming pool, or exercise classes, shop for a gym almost as carefully as you'd shop for a spouse. In either case, the wrong one will make you miserable. Most important is finding a friendly gym. Lots of them seem friendly until they get your money, and then you can't get so much as a towel if your life depends on it. Don't join a club that won't let you have a two-week trial membership to get a feel for the place—the facilities, the other members, and the staff.

If there is even one knowledgeable, compassionate person there who is willing to answer your questions and help you out, go during his or her shift and consider yourself blessed. I stayed at one health club for nine years because a particular instructor and trainer, Toni Rader, had such a radiant presence I'd come to an aerobics class simply because she was teaching it. Toni had her priorities straight: they call this a health club because you're supposed to get healthier by coming here. It's not about staring at yourself in the mirror and having a better butt than the next person.

If you're noticeably overweight, don't join some elite gym full of model and athlete types. It's hard to be happy about losing five pounds when everybody else looks like a centerfold. And try to find a place that isn't so body-conscious that anorexia starts looking normal. Weight obsession is the flip side of food obsession, and you're striving for balance.

Often women do better at women-only gyms. That way you don't have to worry about sexual tension (or feeling that what you may regard as your currently unsexy body is interfering with the sexual tension). Besides, the weight machines at a women-only place are scaled for women's bodies and don't imply that you ought to be bench-pressing three hundred pounds.

Finally, if you have options about where you'll join, choose a place that feels right. This is a more ethereal concept than most people have in mind when looking for somewhere to exercise, but I promise you: if you sign up for a year and the place doesn't feel right to you, you'll be paying dues for nine months during which you will never darken the door of that gym.

A health club—or anywhere else for that matter—feels right when you perceive it as welcoming. It feels right when the lighting suits you and, if natural light is important to you, there are big, clean windows. It feels right when the colors and the decor and the smell in the locker room remind you of either something good or nothing at all. And it feels right when there are at least a few people there who have something in common with you. If you can find a place like this, you'll know why they call it a club, because you'll fit right in.

38

GROOM YOURSELF

LIKE A RACEHORSE

⁓

When you commit to grooming yourself like a prize racehorse,

whether you feel like a prize on a particular day or not, you give

yourself a venue for treating yourself in lovely ways.

"THERE ARE TWO KINDS OF WOMEN," my grandmother used to tell me, "workhorses and racehorses. You decide which one you want to be." I think men can be workhorses and racehorses, too. The former is valued only for getting a job done, the latter for doing it with grace and style. The first step toward becoming a racehorse is to groom yourself like one. Fat people have an undeserved reputation for being lazy, even dirty. Fight the prejudice—and feel terrific about yourself—by being not just clean and neat but also impeccably groomed, like a racehorse.

Certainly a lot of people of all weights and sizes are well groomed as a matter of course. They were raised that way and it stuck. When I was overeating, though, my grooming habits followed my eating habits. When I binged, I didn't take care of my body any more than I had to for holding down a job so I could buy more food. When I dieted, I was a veritable Greta Grooming, part of the all-or-nothing mentality that so often characterizes a binge/diet lifestyle. Either way, because I had failed to develop consistent self-care habits during my childhood and youth, I had to be *conscious* of showering every day, brushing my teeth, taking my makeup off at night—basic routines that should have been second nature.

If taking care of your physical self comes naturally to you, you don't need this reminder, but if it doesn't, be aware every day that you are fully worthy of being groomed like a racehorse. (Even if you weren't, the people around you deserve to be in the presence of someone who is well groomed and pulled together.) Taking good care of your physical needs—from basic self-care to manicures and pedicures and facials when you get the chance—will support your weight loss efforts in a variety of ways. It will:

• *Help you befriend your body.* We care more for anything we take care of. A history of being overweight can put a person and his body at odds, as if there were two entities present, each playing for a different team. As you take care of your body, though, your physical and mental selves form a team of their own. You start to realize that what benefits your body benefits you, and vice versa.

• *Establish binge-proof habits.* No one has determined for certain whether bouts of overeating result in binge scenarios (poor grooming, lack of interest in life, a sense of hopelessness), or whether binge scenarios result in bouts of overeating. Establishing conscientious self-care habits may put you in a stronger position to refrain from turning to food.

- *Increase the integrity in your life.* If you always take a shower in the morning, wash your hair every other day, and do your nails on Thursday night, you have a code of behavior you can be proud of. If you maintain this code of behavior, even if your eating gets shaky, it will be easier to bring the food back into line because you won't feel that you've lost everything. And if you eat something you wished you hadn't and still take a shower, wash your hair, and do your nails, it's far less likely that an indiscretion will turn into a lost weekend.

- *Provide a way to give gifts to yourself.* In a period of self-hatred, taking a bath is a chore. In a period of self-approval, it's a treat. When you commit to grooming yourself like a prize racehorse, whether you feel like a prize on a particular day or not, you give yourself a venue for treating yourself in lovely ways. Department store cosmetics departments don't cover acres because people need grape-flavored body balm, shine serum for their hair, bath salts from the Dead Sea, or even soap-on-a-rope. That stuff is there because we like it. It's a harmless luxury you deserve to enjoy to whatever degree makes you happy.

39

STAND UP FOR YOURSELF

⌒

Don't let people put you down for your weight—

not anyone, not ever.

DON'T LET PEOPLE PUT YOU down for your weight—not anyone, not ever. If this happens and confrontation is not your style, at least talk about what took place with someone who understands or write about it in your journal until it doesn't hurt anymore.

A friend of mine who gained some twenty-five pounds during college got to the point where she dreaded talking to her own father, whom she loved very much, because he always asked if she was losing weight, if she was watching her diet, and the like. Invariably, after one of those conversations, she would assuage her feelings of shame with peanuts or pretzels. This went on for several years until she started dating a man who called it to her attention after overhearing a couple of these phone calls from Dad. "He has no right to make you feel this way," her boyfriend told her. "Just tell him nicely that he can help you more by not bringing it up."

It had never occurred to her that she had this right. The next time her father called and started on the inevitable "How much weight did you lose this week?" she said, "Dad, I love you, and I know your heart is in the right place, but your asking about my weight hurts my feelings and doesn't help me. Please don't do it anymore." Her father assured her that he had only been trying to help and that, of course, he would stop talking about it. Which he did.

My friend began using many of the techniques we're discussing here: eating healthfully, not depriving herself, and treating herself to life's many delicacies, not just food. Slowly and without undue effort, she lost the twenty-five pounds. In fifteen years, they've never come back.

Don't let anyone put you down for your weight: not friends, relatives, or strangers. There are far worse failings than overeating. It just happens to be one with obvious consequences, making overweight people ripe for others' pontificating—the well-meaning ones like my friend's father and the intentionally cruel ones as well. Don't put up with it. You're too valuable.

40

THINK "STILL LIFE"

Plan your meals as if each were a still life painting.

WHEN I WAS WRITING a section on food for my book about inner beauty, *Lit from Within*, I came up with the notion of eating a "still life diet." No, this isn't going *on* a diet; it's a visual cue for designing a way of eating that respects your body, your aesthetic sense, and yourself as a person worth treating like a king or queen. The idea is to plan your meals as if each were a still life painting. The foods chosen for the Old Masters' still life renderings were fresh and beautiful. This is a delightful way to create fresh, beautiful meals.

Something you will invariably find absent in a still life painting is packaging—no boxes, no cans, no microwave-safe trays. Our society is fond of packaging everything, not just what we eat. When I was visiting a Tibetan refugee family in rural India, a salient feature of the household was that there was no trash receptacle. These resourceful people didn't generate any trash. Embarrassed, I stuffed my Western world rubbish into my suitcase—water bottles, used Kleenex, the foil encasements of my antibacterial wipes.

After this foray into refuse smuggling, I thought about our cultural dependence on wrappings of various sorts and realized that, when it comes to food, some of the healthiest ones available, fresh fruits and vegetables, come packaging free. Many other good foods—rice, dried beans, raw nuts—are often sold in bulk so you can scoop them out of bins or barrels. This is the stuff of still life dining.

If you look closely at these paintings (make a point of looking for some when you visit an art museum—see Chapter 87), you will be aware that in lieu of Styrofoam and aluminum the food is shown on lovely plates and platters and the beverages in wonderful pitchers, whether of rustic pottery or fine silver. If you choose to serve meals deserving a spot in a gallery, use the good dishes, even when you're having soup and salad by yourself. Who were you saving them for anyway?

Another hallmark of the still life approach is that all the foods in those paintings, whether of vegetable or animal origin, came from nature with minimal modification between farm and table. Natural foods, especially those that grow in gardens and on trees, are lovely to look at; no wonder people like to paint them. And because we eat with our eyes as well as our taste buds, artful foods artfully presented feed us in more ways than one.

41

Never Punish Yourself

⌒

Getting through childhood, adulthood,

and old age can be challenging enough without

volunteering to be your own worst enemy.

There are all sorts of ways to punish yourself for eating too much, weighing too much, or in some other way not measuring up. You could starve yourself—or stuff yourself. You could berate yourself—or run an extra mile. You could keep yourself from buying a new outfit until you're thinner—or refrain from going out with your friends because you don't look good enough. The possibilities are endless, a real masochist's playground.

A vindictive attitude toward yourself, however, will not help you one bit. Instead, do the best you can. If you fall short, do better next time. Getting through childhood, adulthood, and old age can be challenging enough without volunteering to be your own worst enemy. My grandmother used to say, "Life is a school." Let yourself learn. That's what you're here for. This is not an excuse for giving up, giving in, slacking off, or deluding yourself. It's simply allowing yourself the room you need to get better.

If you've been punitive in the past, watch what you say to yourself, both aloud and inside your head. When "You're so stupid" or some similar sentiment surfaces, defuse it. One of my friends says "Cancel!"—right out loud—when a put-down crosses her lips. She then rephrases it as something like "You're so human— bless your heart."

Watch for subtle ways in which you punish yourself for actual or imagined infractions of the guidelines you've set for yourself or the silent "rules" you've picked up elsewhere. Don't fail on purpose, and in the food arena, keep yourself in the safety of this day so a setback is less likely. But when you do disappoint yourself— whether in your choice of food, the amount you eat, or something that has nothing to do with eating—treat yourself the way you would treat your best friend under similar circumstances. You wouldn't say, "It's okay: why don't you have a big, juicy burger and a pound of cole slaw?" But neither would you say, "You are really a piece of work. How could you be such an idiot?"

Be a friend to yourself. Learn the lessons life presents. And in the meantime, let yourself grow, heal, renew, rejuvenate, and triumph.

42

GET A SUPPORT SYSTEM

⌒

Seek the counsel of persons who have tread this path

before you and accomplished what you want to do yourself.

They can be the next best thing to guardian angels.

I RECOMMEND OVEREATERS Anonymous in Chapter 20 because I believe it to be the preeminent support system for compulsive overeaters. Even if you don't think of yourself as "compulsive," you may want to try a few meetings and see if there might be some valuable support for you there. If OA is not for you, do put together some kind of support system for yourself.

You have to be able to talk things out—hurts, questions, decisions, dilemmas. Civilians, people who have never had a weight problem, may love you to pieces, but they're virtually worthless when it comes to understanding what you've been through and what you're doing to change things. Don't frustrate yourself by expecting people to understand who never will. Instead, get yourself a group of allies (in person or online) who are using some of the same tools you are to reach a long-term healthy body size. You can find them in an established organization or gather them from people you already know.

Characteristics to look for in the people who'll support you in this are kindness, honesty, and a generous spirit that leaves jealousy and pettiness outside the door. Talk with them. Compare notes. Walk or exercise together. Pour out your heart when necessary. And seek the counsel of persons who have tread this path before you and accomplished what you want to do yourself. They can be the next best thing to guardian angels. When the going gets tough, you want to know there are individuals you can reach out to who will know what you're talking about and be able to help.

Shortly before I embarked on the path of losing weight for the last time, I joined a generic support group (not specifically for eating problems) in which people were supposed to pair up and listen with "positive regard" to one another. The third or fourth time I was there I was paired with a woman about my age. I listened to her talk. When it was my turn, I started to tell her about the stresses in my life and how I'd been eating over them. "Then I ate half a box of Grape-Nuts," I said—and she burst out laughing. She apologized, but even then she was stifling a giggle. If I'd said half a box of chocolates, she might have contained herself; I mean, we've all heard about people who overeat chocolates. But the idea that I could stuff myself on cereal that has a wholesome, healthy reputation went straight to her funny bone.

I never went back, but that experience taught me the value of sharing selectively, choosing what information to offer to what person. When food is the problem, you need to have people in place around you who understand that food can indeed be a problem—the way you might discuss a job predicament with someone in your industry instead of with someone who knows nothing about it.

It is also advisable when looking for support in becoming fit from within that you depend on more than one person. Weight loss statistics are sobering. Should your friend be among those who give up, you want enough additional support that you won't throw in the towel, too. Part of your support system can be a caring physician, dietitian, or trainer. Just be sure everyone in your support network is truly supportive. You will need them.

43

LEARN TO COOK—
OR TO COOK DIFFERENTLY

◦━◦

It's difficult to maintain a healthy weight

if you can't do some basic cooking.

NOT LONG AGO I SPOKE on food and wellness for a group of physical therapists. One of the participants shared with me that the night before their last office potluck, a bright young colleague, fresh out of university, had called to ask, "What's 'dice'?" That word in the potato salad recipe had tripped her up. Unfortunately, her unfamiliarity with the basics of food preparation is not unusual. The average mom hasn't been based in the kitchen for over a generation, and mandatory home economics classes went the way of the dinosaur even earlier. As a result, a lot of us are clueless about getting food on the table.

It's difficult to maintain a healthy weight if you can't do some basic cooking. This is true even if you're young (you're not *too* young), if you're male (so are some of the world's greatest chefs), or if you live in New York City (the delivery people could go on strike).

When you do learn to cook, learn to do it in a healthful way, using modest amounts of oil, light sauces, and plenty of vegetables. Take a class or get some instruction from a friend who knows how to cook healthy, tasty food. Do the same if you know how to cook but the way you do it is more of a hindrance than a help. When I was a little girl in Missouri, there was a jar of bacon drippings on the stove, shortening was always in the cupboard, and white flour, butter, and sugar were what my grandmother referred to as *staples*. I had to unlearn that way of doing things and replace it with one that serves me better. You can, too.

A caveat here: if you're fixated on food to such an extent that even reading about it in a cookbook seems unsafe right now, put this off. Keep your meals uncomplicated, whether you're eating in or out. You'll know when the time is right for perusing cookbooks. I'd been eating well for about three months before I felt that the next step for me was to get some healthy cookbooks and expand my culinary scope.

In those early years of sane eating, I developed something of a reputation as a chef. These days other things interest me much more than cooking. When I do cook, my objective is to come up with a civilized but unpretentious meal. When I have a choice, though, I'd rather go out. It's being over fifty, friends tell me. They say you can reach a point at which you've fed people long enough and you'd rather let somebody else cook so there's more time to feed your soul. That sounds right to me, but whether I cook or let Luigi at the pasta place do it, we both know how. And that knowledge is power.

44

Treat Yourself to
Therapeutic Massage

There is nothing like massage to get you back in your body if

you've been living from the neck up.

A FIRST-RATE WAY TO nurture a body is with massage. Trained massage therapists work on all kind of bodies, and their commitment is to help each one relax, unwind, and heal. People concerned with food and weight need this nurturing touch most of all. Whether we're markedly obese, somewhat overweight, or simply feel fat (because we just ate or because it's raining or because we don't know how to feel any other way), we can wrongly believe that our bodies are untouchable and undeserving. Massage can help turn this around.

There is also nothing like massage to get you back into your body if you've been living from the neck up. This happens a lot if you're not thrilled with how your body looks or feels, or if you want to eat what you want to eat and not be aware of the discomfort afterward. Massage offers a gentle invitation to get back inside your skin—all of it. Furthermore, it's a great way to feel physical enough that exercise starts to look attractive, even if it hasn't for quite some time.

If you can afford a weekly or every-other-week massage, get one. (Don't write off the idea immediately with "I haven't got the money." Budgets can be tweaked and juggled. It may be time to tweak yours in favor of some self-nurture.) Getting a massage even once a month is better than never. You may want to schedule a regular massage just after your monthly check-in on the scale. This way you can convince yourself that, regardless of the verdict from the almighty weighing machine, you are fully deserving of healing touch and pleasurable sensations.

45

GET ALL SIX TASTES IN EVERY MEAL

Give your body the tastes that tell it it's been fed.

ACCORDING TO THE INDIAN healing system of Ayurveda, one reason people overeat is that most of us do not get all six tastes—sweet, salty, bitter, sour, pungent, and astringent—in all our meals (our main meals anyway—breakfast can be exempt). In the West, we favor sweet and salty tastes, and anyone who has ever gone on an eating binge can tell you it was probably on sweet foods, salty foods, or a pendulum swing from one to the other. For the body to sense that it is getting what it needs, and feel satisfied as a result, it requires not only sweet and salty flavors but also the bitter taste (leafy greens, citrus rind, the spices turmeric and fenugreek), the pungent taste (onions, garlic, cayenne, ginger), the astringent taste (beans, apples, cabbage, potatoes), and the sour taste (lemon, pickles, yogurt, tomatoes, plums).

Including all six tastes in every lunch and supper causes you to eat a wide variety of foods and therefore get optimal nutrition. In planting within us the desire for the full complement of tastes, nature made certain we would try to obtain all the necessary nutrients thousands of years before anyone had heard of a vitamin or a phytochemical.

Still, it's sometimes hard in our busy lives to get this much variety. To fill in missing tastes, my Ayurvedic doctor advised me to have the Indian condiment chutney on the table. Traditional chutney includes all the tastes and is a delicious side dish at any meal—sort of like cranberry sauce at Thanksgiving. You can find chutney at Indian groceries or in the foreign foods aisle of any major supermarket. There are several varieties—mango, apple, apricot, peach—so you can vary the ones you choose, but any chutney is supposed to fill in missing tastes.

No taste on the tongue and no food in the stomach will appease inner yearnings, emotional longings, or spiritual emptiness. There is no getting around the need to do the work necessary to address these. But make things easier on yourself in this very basic sense by giving your body the tastes that tell it it's been fed.

46

HAVE PLENTY OF
HEALTHY FOOD AROUND

~

Assure the part of yourself that may worry about it that you'll

always have more than enough food available.

IF YOU'VE EVER WONDERED how much truth is in the old saying "Out of sight, out of mind," keep healthy food out of the house for a week or two. Unless you're so used to eating nutritious foods that your body goes into alarm mode without them, not having healthy food around could cause you to forget that it exists at all. White bread, lunch meat, potato chips, and vanilla wafers can start to look like a balanced diet when that's all that's on hand.

Instead, arrange to see healthy food when you walk into the kitchen and when you open the refrigerator door. When supplies run low, get used to finishing the sentence "We're out of . . ." with foods that grew, foods that have the decency to rot when they're old, foods that can do something for your body besides fill your stomach.

Some people who have had trouble with overeating are afraid of not having enough to eat. A few were actually deprived of food as children. For most heavy people, though, there is no obvious explanation for this exaggerated fear of being without food. Whatever the reason, give yourself the comfort of having plenty of good food around.

Maintain a well-stocked pantry and freezer. Have a bowl or basket of fruit out where you can see it so you'll remember to eat the two to five pieces a day that nutritionists recommend for optimum health. Have fresh vegetables, already washed and cut up, in airtight bags in the fridge. I know it costs more to buy them this way. Please: spend the money. This is no place to economize, especially if your eating has resembled the kind I used to do. That will cost you lots more—in surreptitious shopping and possibly future medical bills—than you could possibly spend on carrots and cauliflower that someone else was kind enough to wash and chop for you.

Have plenty of healthy food around. Assure the part of yourself that may worry about it that you'll always have more than enough food available. You'll be okay. You've got yourself in your corner.

Watch Naturally Thin People

The naturally thin are just normal-looking people who

eat what they need, enjoy what they eat,

and don't worry about their weight.

Our culture is so thin-obsessed that it is sometimes hard to find a thin person who is willing to admit that she doesn't "work at it." Not being on a diet or somehow watching one's weight can, in some circles, make a person a social outcast. ("I hate you" is a common comment such people hear from their purported friends.) Still, be on the lookout for the naturally thin. They aren't necessarily the ultrathin. They're just normal-looking people who eat what they need, enjoy what they eat, and don't worry about their weight.

The naturally thin don't go on at length about either food or body size; they have other interests. Most appreciate good food; a few consider eating a necessary but not particularly splendid part of life. Some eat heartily; others are downright finicky. Either way, when the meal is over they're on to other things.

The naturally thin are more interested in the people they're with than the food on their plate. If the food isn't great, it doesn't ruin their evening. They rarely eat every bite. They may leave the box of leftovers on the table at the restaurant, or they didn't ask to have them boxed in the first place. They don't seem to need much density in their food. That is, they may actually *prefer* sherbet to ice cream or a shot of espresso to a white chocolate mocha with caramel. They realize that certain foods are more nutritious than others, but they don't rank foods on an ethical scale from virtuous to demonic. They simply don't give food that much power or that much thought.

If they drink soda, the naturally thin almost always drink regular soda instead of the diet stuff. I am not condoning either sort: one is full of sugar, and the other contains questionable chemical sweeteners. There are lots of better things to drink than soda. Still, naturally trim people almost always opt for the real thing, because it tastes better.

Just as they don't understand why someone would consume what they consider to be foul-tasting cola, it doesn't make sense to them that anyone would want the discomfort of overeating. They're like teetotalers and moderate drinkers who can't figure out how being drunk could possibly be worth suffering a hangover. Overeating perplexes them. As a naturally thin woman commented to me at a Thanksgiving dinner, "I just don't get it: I can't eat any more on Thanksgiving than any other day."

Find these people. Watch them. Listen to what they say. Their laissez-faire attitude about eating may not seem natural to you for a long time, and maybe never completely. But if you model your behavior after theirs—allowing, of course, for individual differences like a food allergy or a problem with sugar—you will be acting like a naturally slim person. Eventually, you'll even feel like one to a great extent. It's okay that it's not 100 percent. It's good to remember that any one of us could always go back to our old ways and be fat again. People like you and me can emulate the naturally thin as role models. We can learn from them, and we can look like them. We just need to be grateful for what they can take for granted.

48

HIRE A PHYSICIAN
WHO RESPECTS YOU

~

What you need from your health provider is not

a magic bullet but a magical attitude,

one of respect for you as a valuable human being.

IF YOU'RE JUST A FEW pounds overweight, the situation is mostly cosmetic and your doctor may not even get involved. If you are greatly overweight, though—especially if you have weight-related disorders like high blood pressure, arthritis, diabetes, or a prediabetic condition—your doctor is likely to sound like a broken record: "You've got to lose weight. You've got to lose weight. You've got to . . ." This long-suffering physician is most likely well-meaning, but if the doctor has never had a weight problem, he or she can only give you the party line: "Eat less fat. Eat fewer calories. Exercise three or four times a week."

It is laughable that an educated professional would assume you don't already know that. The predicament is not that you don't know what to do but that you haven't been able to do it. Few doctors have the answer. What you need from your health provider is not a magic bullet but a magical attitude, one of respect for you as a valuable human being with much to give and much to live for. You need a doctor who says something like, "Ms. Brown, you know as well as I do that you need to lose at least thirty pounds. We both know this is not easy. I want to help you all I can, but frankly it's frustrating because most of my patients have such a hard time losing weight and keeping it off. What do you think I can do to help you?"

If you find this Marcus Welby clone, you can tell him or her what you really need. Is it nutritional counseling from a qualified dietitian? A referral to a therapist so you can deal with the inner issues that may be at the root of your overeating? A support group recommendation? A monthly appointment to come in and weigh so you can get rid of the dreaded bathroom scale? An exercise class for people who don't yet have buns of forged metal?

Probably the greatest help a doctor can be is to respect you as an equal, intelligent, responsible human being. If the one you have doesn't do that, see what you can do about getting a replacement. Interview this person when both of you are sitting up and fully clothed. Credentials can be impressive, but if you sense that Dr. Harvard Yale Hopkins is not truly interested in your well-being, interview somebody else.

You might ask straight out how this physician feels about treating overweight patients. If his or her answer reflects understanding and compassion as well as a grasp of the medical aspects, you just might have unearthed yourself a gem. If he or she understands nutrition—not just the chemistry of it but how it translates into what's for lunch—you're lucky. And if your intuitive sense of the doctor you're interviewing is that he is someone you could turn to, talk to, and trust, you've found your man. Or your woman. This is someone who will be there for you as you make progress and if you have trouble. It's someone who will respect you in either case and will stand by you through the hard times until they aren't hard anymore.

49

CHANNEL YOUR SENSITIVITY

Sensitivity is an admirable quality. . . . The problem comes in not knowing how to control its intensity or channel its course.

IF I HAD A DOLLAR FOR every time I heard "You've got to stop being so sensitive" while growing up, I'd buy you a car. A good one. I was a sensitive kid, and I am sensitive to this day. I believe many men and women who have, or have had, weight problems are more sensitive than a lot of other people are. Although the specifics differ from person to person, those of us with this trait are likely to cry at movies and weddings and the library. We may feel sorely injured by slights, rudeness, and criticism—devastated if these come from an authority figure and pretty well bummed if they come from a stranger on the subway who would be back in Bellevue if there were enough beds available.

We seem to feel everybody else's pain, and we feel our own so acutely we've used food to try to feel it less. (Indeed, a great many people go back to overeating because they're not prepared to deal with the feelings that come up when food is no longer pushing them down.) Some of us are so sensitive to the troubles of the world that friends see us as saints in the making. Other friends describe us as intuitive and therefore exceptionally wise. We like being exceptional, because as sensitive people, we are sent flying by compliments the way insults can send us crashing.

It's not bad, being sensitive. In fact, sensitivity is an admirable quality. If it replaced disinterest on a global scale, we'd all be better off. The problem comes in not knowing how to control its intensity or channel its course. Being sensitive to the needs of others is a virtue unless you're so sensitive that you cannot respond to those needs, because you're always saying something like "It's so awful—I just can't think about it." And if you become so troubled by the amount of pain on this planet that you can no longer experience the joy that thrives alongside it, you forfeit much of your ability to make a difference. Genuinely helpful people live full lives and, without denying the suffering that exists, find something every day to be glad about.

When your sensitivity is focused on yourself, it's hard for others to get close. It can take you so far down the "poor me" track that you end up spending most of your time hobbling about with hurt feelings. Before long self-pity moves in. Then grudges take root and grow like weeds in an untended garden. This is a red-alert zone for anybody who's had a checkered history with food. Being in the throes of "poor me" is one step away from standing in front of the refrigerator and eating peanut butter out of the jar.

And any overeater who believes she has been so maligned by other people or life in general that she has every right to lug around a satchel of resentments should just cash in her assets, buy a fried chicken franchise, and never leave the kitchen. That is at least a direct route to where hypersensitivity, self-pity, and righteous indignation were going to get her anyway.

Let yourself feel things. Be grateful that you do. Use your support people and your spiritual connection to help you when it's hard. Right whatever wrongs are in your power to affect, whether by offering a hand, mailing a check, or taking care of yourself if the person in need at the moment happens to be you. But just as you're learning to stop eating when you've had enough food, and to stop losing weight when you don't need to lose any more, you can learn—if this applies to you—to stop bemoaning how awful things are. Change what you can. Pray for what you can't. And make the world better by being as happy as you can be today. I'm convinced that when anyone feels the least bit blissful, there is a ripple effect that benefits the rest of us. The next person to do this service to humanity may as well be you.

BE CAREFUL WITH CAFFEINE

~

Those for whom a little caffeine yields a big rush find that is a

temporary appetite suppressant. . . . When the short-term effect

is over, however, the appetite can return with a vengeance.

COFFEE, TEA, AND DIET COLA—ah, the glorious "freebies" of almost every diet for the past forty years! But watch it with caffeine. People have vastly different tolerance levels for it. Some hardly notice a buzz. Those for whom a little caffeine yields a big rush find that it is a temporary appetite suppressant. (This is why it's a common ingredient in over-the-counter diet aids.) When the short-term effect is over, however, the appetite can return with a vengeance.

Like drinking alcohol, caffeine consumption is part of human culture around the world. In places where coffee is uncommon, people make beverages from caffeine-containing herbs like maté, or they make the tea really strong so the morning lift you get in Bombay is not that different from the one you get in Boston.

Despite its popularity, caffeine is, pharmacologically, a stimulant to the heart and central nervous system. This isn't all bad.

Some studies have shown that caffeine makes people sharper mentally (until the effect wears off), and it's a rare individual who can't credit coffee or Coke for getting them through the day after a sleepless night. The problem arises when we need caffeine to get through every day or use it as a substitute for sleeping enough at night. If we do this for a long time, we can end up with weakened adrenal glands and an overall sluggishness that makes us look and feel older than we have to.

Whether or not you drink coffee, or how strong you take your tea, is a personal matter. If it doesn't seem like a problem, it probably isn't. I've found a distinct correlation in myself between binge behavior and too much caffeine. Sugar and refined carbohydrates, as well as large quantities of just about anything edible, are soporific. They make you tired. They can also "numb you out" mentally, taking the edge off anxiety. When I drink more than a little coffee, I feel the kind of agitation and uneasiness that I used to eat to tone down. I've heard some other overeaters, although certainly not all, say the same thing.

For the most part, then, I confine my caffeine intake to drinking tea—not too strong, and not pots and pots, but enough to get that little push without going overboard. (Green tea—the same plant as black tea but harvested earlier—has a light, distinctive flavor, less caffeine than regular tea, and it's loaded with powerful antioxidants and with flavonoids that boost metabolism.)

The fact is, caffeine is addictive: people who quit cold turkey go through headaches, irritability, dizziness—symptoms similar to withdrawal from other drugs. I choose to have some of it with the full understanding that I am ingesting an addictive and somewhat mood-altering substance. If you drink coffee, tea, and cola—or use medications like Anacin or Excedrin that contain caffeine—you need to understand this, too. See how your caffeine intake correlates with what you eat or what you want to eat. Make any alterations necessary to further your cause.

51

TAP INTO YOUR COURAGE

Courage travels with faith. When you're counting on

a Higher Power or a higher purpose, you've got

a light to help you through the dark places.

COURAGE IS NOT RESERVED for those who save lives or make headlines. We all have it, and we've displayed it in our everyday lives. If we were in circumstances that called for remarkable courage, most of us would have that, too. In those situations, adrenaline and impulse combine with courage to enable ordinary people to do extraordinary things. The courage you need for most days, though, is the kind they don't give medals for. It's the courage to confront a superior on an issue you cannot in good conscience let slide. It's the courage you need to take up for someone weak who needs a champion, or to face a fear like speaking before an audience, or having dinner at your folks' house and saying no to Aunt Genevieve's fabled coconut cake.

Courage is an odd quality in that you might have a great deal of it in one area and virtually none in another. I once walked straight up to a drunken wild man who was abusing a puppy. I also once called my boyfriend in a panic and convinced him to come to my house to catch a cricket—a cricket!—because I was so afraid of bugs.

In the eating arena, it can be scary to go places where there are a lot of your favorite foods, or where the food is different from what you're used to, or where you'll be around people you're not comfortable with. Remember: food is not an attack force. It won't get in your mouth if you don't put it there. Don't seek out intimidating situations just to prove you can deal with them, but when one is in your path, do your best to face your fear so it won't alter your course.

If you're an overeater, the most meaningful action you can take to increase your courage is to keep food that has no business in your mouth out of it. You may have no idea how brave you are until you've sat out the urge to consume a cafeteria. You may have said, aloud or to yourself, "I eat because I'm happy, I eat because I'm sad, I eat because I'm lonely, I eat because I'm mad . . . ," but have you ever said, "I eat because I'm afraid"? I think more emotional eating goes on because of fear than any of those other things. It takes courage to face the world, deal with other people, and take the risks required to create a better life. If cheese Danish could reliably provide that courage, I'd say, "Pick up half a dozen." But they can't provide it—not well anyway, and not for long.

Beyond abstaining from using food as a courage crutch, cut down on fear by taking each day as it comes. Deal with your various stressors (relationships, overscheduling, finances) and be so good to yourself on ordinary days that you'll be up to the challenge of the unnerving ones. If you're facing a trying food situation, take this book along with you, as well as a couple of phone numbers of people you can call when you find out that "brunch" won't be served until 2:00 P.M., it's 11:00 now, and you're already starving. Together you'll figure out exactly what to do.

Always, whether you can reach an understanding friend or not, stay close to the God of your understanding. Prayer is a useful exercise, in both foxholes and buffet lines. When you get used to using it, there will always be two of you when it's time to face something difficult—and one of you will be perfect. Whether you feel you need more courage to deal with food or with other issues, you can't escape the fact that courage travels with faith. When you're counting on a Higher Power or a higher purpose, you've got a light to help you through the dark places.

STOP COMPARING

Comparing is a game that nobody wins. Besides, in a spiritual

sense, we're connected to everybody else anyway.

A COMPASSIONATE REMINDER: you are not a supermodel, and this is not seven years ago when you lost that twenty-five pounds. You're you, and this is now, and life is, in spite of its hardships, good. You miss out on way too much of the good stuff when you compare yourself to other people or your former self. It also discounts who you are right now.

Stop comparing yourself to friends, strangers, and earlier editions of yourself. Comparing is a game that nobody wins. Besides, in a spiritual sense, we're connected to everybody else anyway. Charting who is better and who is worse keeps people separated and oneness an alien concept. Do away with it. Refrain from juvenile contests about who's losing more weight or who's losing it faster. Support your friends who are trying to do this, too, and know that you deserve the same unconditional backing, whether they know how to give it or not. And when anyone you know has a triumph in any area of life, celebrate with him. Be part of the exhilaration of somebody else's time in the sun. Blessings are contagious anyway: be there for other people's and watch them rub off.

Stop comparing yourself to models and entertainment icons, too. It's their job to look the way they do, at least on camera. If you enjoy fashion and beauty magazines as I do, look at them for fun, for ideas to spur your own sense of style, and as artistic explorations into photography and design, not as arbiters of how you're supposed to look. These publications are an imaginative blend of fantasy and commerce. Their writers and editors are regular people who come in all sizes. If their work inspires you to treat yourself like somebody special, they've succeeded. If it doesn't, read something different.

However you feel about yourself today, and whether or not you believe you deserve it, make a commitment to taking loving care of yourself as you are right now. Savor the time you spend with the people who matter and on the parts of your life that make you so happy you could start dancing in the streets. There is no need to compare yourself to anybody else, because you are one of a kind. Other people have every right to be beautiful, handsome, rich, powerful, madly in love, or mildly in ecstasy. So do you.

BE WILLING TO CHANGE
AT THE DESIRE LEVEL

"Enough" is a territory practicing overeaters rarely visit. You get

there when you're willing to let your desires reflect your needs.

AT THE CORE OF BECOMING fit from within is change from the inside out, change at the desire level. I can honestly tell you that what I *need* to eat to keep my body the size it likes to be is precisely what I *want* to eat. I am no paragon of willpower. I eat what I want and plenty of it. It's just that what I want today is different than it was eighteen years ago. A while back, for instance, my daughter brought in the only nonpremium chocolate that I consider good enough to eat. She asked if I wanted some. I did: one section. It was yummy. "Do you want more?" she asked. "No thanks." And that was the truth. I'd had enough.

"Enough" is a territory practicing overeaters rarely visit. You get there when you're willing to let your desires reflect your needs. It will take some time. In the interim, do what you know is expedient, whether you want to or not. You'll sometimes need to say,

"No, I don't think I'll have another piece; I'm really full" when you are actually thinking, "Another piece would be a ticket to heaven." This is in the esteemed tradition of "Fake it till you make it." Eventually, you'll hardly ever need to fake it, because your desires themselves will have changed.

You cannot force this or speed it up. It will come as the result of going through this process: including a spiritual component, caring for yourself, not eating for the wrong reasons, and choosing quality food when the reasons are right. This will divert your route toward a different end point. While before that end point might have been a size 8, or 130 pounds, or being skinnier than your sister, it's now changing your mind-set so that what you want and what you need become synonymous.

As you trust in God or your higher self to get you through without extra food, and as you practice the disciplines that lead to a quieter mind, you'll become more willing to do what's good for you. From willingness comes desire. This is how you'll grow into wanting what's good for you. You will have changed at the desire level. This is the closest thing to a guarantee anyone can have that worrying about weight has been relegated to history and you can work on other things.

54

When People Notice You've Lost Weight, Change the Subject

⌒

When people rave about your weight loss,

"Uh-huh" is the only answer you owe them.

PEOPLE LOVE TO TELL YOU when they see you losing weight, and they love to talk behind your back when they see you gain it. You diffuse the intensity around this issue by refusing to allow your weight or your food choices to be a topic of idle conversation. Someone at work, for instance, may wax poetic with something like "Oh, my God! You look fabulous. Turn around. Let me see you. This is incredible. How much have you lost? What are you doing? You look so awesome." Downplay her excitement (envy?) with something simple like "Yeah, I've lost some weight. Nothing special—I'm just eating a little healthier."

You may in fact be praying five times a day that you won't succumb to your old patterns. You may have joined a support group and a gym, be eating vegetables you hadn't heard of six months ago, and feel that you are revolutionizing your life. You probably are. It's nobody's business, least of all the peripheral people in your life. When they rave about your weight loss, "Uh-huh" is the only answer you owe them. You have a right to your privacy. Even when someone is paying you a compliment, it doesn't always have to be about your body. There is much more to you than that.

In addition, there are implications here that reach beyond you and your weight loss. Women, in particular, need to be recognized for more than physical attributes. We didn't become a weight-obsessed, appearance-oriented society because people were discussing literature, art, and current affairs. When you shift the focus away from your body, you take the focus off bodies in general. You've made life a little easier for your daughters and for every other woman in the Western world.

Discover Yoga

⌒

Yoga addresses the whole person. It improves the state of the

mind as well as the shape of the body.

I WAS INITIALLY ATTRACTED to yoga because it was the first physical discipline I'd ever heard of that acknowledged that human beings have minds and souls as well as abs and glutes. It was also gentler than other exercises I'd tried, and when I got up my nerve to go to a class, the people there were of all ages and sizes. Not only that: they seemed content.

Yoga can be a total fitness package that increases your endurance, strength, and—here is where it really shines—flexibility. No one is too large, too stiff, too old, or in any other way not right for beginning to practice traditional hatha yoga (*hatha* refers to physical yoga, not one of the more mystical disciplines). Its asanas or postures (yoga doesn't use the word *exercise*, a point in its favor) are said to benefit the organs and glands as well as the muscles and joints, so every body function—metabolism of food included—proceeds more efficiently.

Moreover, yoga addresses the whole person. It improves the state of the mind as well as the shape of the body. If you opt to explore it, you may find that as you become more flexible physically, you become more flexible mentally. You'll be able to bend with the circumstances of life the way you bend forward and backward and sideways in yoga class. You may also find, as many a yoga practitioner has, that you make a gradual shift to a healthier, more balanced diet without even realizing that this is happening.

Several styles of yoga are offered today. Shop around until you find a class that suits you. Some are athletic and challenging, even at the beginner's level. Others are slow and easy, equally welcoming to those who are tight from lethargy and to those who are tight from overexertion. If you're a large person in a large city, you may be able to find a class specially designed for plus-size women and men. Otherwise, look for a teacher who is sufficiently skilled, and sufficiently willing, to gear the moves to your ability. Either way, yoga is supposed to be noncompetitive: the "best" person in class is the one on your mat.

Yoga class is, for me, an overhaul of body and mind. It's where I go to limber up, loosen up, energize myself, and relax so completely that I feel better all week, even if I make it to class only one time. Moreover, yoga is based on the principle that mind, body, and spirit are intrinsically connected and each affects the other. Overeating can separate the body from those subtler aspects of our being. Yoga reconnects the parts.

56

ABSTAIN FROM
WEIGHT LOSS GIMMICKS
AND COME-ONS

⌒

Just decide to stop being a consumer of

weight loss paraphernalia.

WEIGHT LOSS IS A $32-BILLION-a-year industry in the United States alone. This mega-business depends on the desperation of people who are overweight or who believe they are. The purveyors of appetite suppressants, exercise gadgets, and diet shakes and bars and powders will thrive without your patronage. Don't let them lure you.

If the no-carb diet, the butt-buster machine, and the herbal appe-zap capsules you tried last year were nothing but a one-week wonder, if they did anything at all, this year's revised, revamped, repackaged versions of the same old stuff aren't miracle cures either. Of course the Barbie-like spokesmodel regaling you with the wonders of this thing is convincing. You'd be convincing, too, if you were getting paid SAG rates plus residuals for saying your spiel.

Just decide to stop being a consumer of weight loss paraphernalia. Buy good food, not diet food. Exercise—without the toys that usually end up selling for five cents on the dollar in a garage sale. Take supplements that can protect your health rather than pills that stress your adrenals in the name of appetite suppression. Use the money you save for some personal pampering, to treat those you love, or to support a cause you believe in. Take care of yourself like someone who is worth caring for. People who accept themselves and respect themselves are not buying this stuff. You don't have to either.

MEDITATE

~

Investing in ten or twenty minutes of silence every day will help

ensure your long-term weight loss by keeping you connected to a

source of power that lets your weary willpower off the hook.

WHEN A MENTOR TOLD me that I would never keep the weight off for good unless I took time every day for meditation, my first thought was "That doesn't burn any calories." I was far from being able to see the whole picture.

Quiet time is essential to give yourself perspective. Investing in ten or twenty minutes of silence every day, preferably in the morning, will help ensure your long-term weight loss by keeping you connected to a source of power that lets your weary willpower off the hook. It will also keep you grounded, more in charge of your life, and less afraid. Quiet time can include prayer, reading spiritual or other uplifting literature, or writing in your journal, but meditation is the crux of it. You've known how to read and write since you were five, and you've known how to pray since the first time you had a nightmare or were afraid of the dark. It's meditation you may want a quick lesson on.

First, don't let the word scare you. Meditation is not some cultish practice that will interfere with your being a good Christian, a good Jew, or a good something else. In fact, meditation, sometimes called *contemplation*, is a part of almost every religion on earth; and if you're not religious, you can meditate in a fully secular fashion and reap its health-promoting, stress-mitigating benefits. Allow me to introduce you to basic meditation for people who don't have time for anything complicated:

Wake up. Go to the bathroom if you need to. Come back to bed and sit cross-legged, leaning against the headboard. If you prefer, sit in a comfortable chair with your feet on the floor. Put your hands in your lap in whatever way is comfortable and notice that you are breathing. Pay attention to the air going into your nostrils and coming out again. There. You're meditating.

If that is too subtle, use a comforting phrase along with your breath. This can be something conventionally spiritual, like "God is—" on the inhalation, "—love" on the exhalation. Or it can just be something positive, such as "All is—" when you inhale, "—well" when you exhale. When other thoughts stop by, be cordial, but don't invite them in. Just keep watching yourself breathe, thinking your phrase. That's all there is to it. Intend to do this every day for the rest of your life. Some days you'll miss. Just don't miss too many.

What you get in return for this simple, exquisite practice is peace of mind, better health, a more pleasant disposition, and a more positive attitude. You also get a technique you can use when you need it—even for two or three minutes, anytime during the day—to calm yourself, improve your mood, or help you sit out a desire to eat in a way you know you'd soon regret. Today I am convinced that the man who told me I couldn't keep weight off without meditation was right. There isn't enough food on earth to fill my soul when it's wanting, but meditation can do it in fifteen minutes.

58

Make the Best Possible Choices from Those Available

"Best" has numerous components: nutrition, taste,

price, aesthetics. It evolves; what you learn

today could make yesterday's best obsolete.

THIS IS THE WISEST DIETARY advice I know: Make the best possible choices from those available. When you have a say in the matter, put yourself in situations where there is an abundance of good choices—markets with colorful produce and fresh, high-quality staples and restaurants where choice foods are used to create lovely dishes. But, life being what it is, many times you won't be in such lofty environs. You'll have to make the best possible choice from a selection that might not be stellar.

At a truck stop in central Iowa one morning, I noticed a pair of travelers with East Coast accents turning their menus over and over as if in doing so they would find something other than variations on the bacon/eggs/pancakes theme. When the waitress went over to take their order, the man of the couple asked, "Do you have anything else—a bagel maybe?" "You seem to be forgetting," the waitress reminded him, "you're in Iowa."

Whether you're at a truck stop in rural Iowa, an exquisite French restaurant, a food court at Disney World, or some prefabricated purveyor of fast food on the interstate, you can't go wrong by choosing the best from what is available. This starts a habit pattern that will pay dividends for you all your life. When you look at a menu, approach the groaning board at a potluck supper, or meander through the supermarket aisles, you will automatically go into discernment mode, selecting the best and leaving the rest. "Best" has numerous components: nutrition, taste, price, aesthetics. It evolves; what you learn today could make yesterday's best obsolete. It is also an individual call.

For example, I'm a vegetarian and I rarely eat eggs. At the Iowa truck stop, I would have—in fact I did have—orange juice, rye toast, and grilled veggies. (I figured if you could get onions, peppers, and tomatoes in an omelet, you could get them on their own.) If you had been there that morning, your best could have been half a cantaloupe and an egg-white omelet with the onions and peppers the cook was already chopping for me. Or you might have drunk tomato juice and coffee and eaten a couple of scrambled eggs and a bowl of oatmeal. Or maybe you'd have ordered a short stack of corncakes because you would have been in Iowa, after all. In this scenario and all others, set your own standards and find your own best.

59

DO THIS STRAIGHT

~

Unlike the prescription amphetamines of my

youth, today's diet drugs won't make you a raving lunatic,

but they may not do much to make you thinner either.

UNLESS YOUR DOCTOR HAS good reason to believe you must be on appetite-suppressing or fat-blocking medication for a prescribed period, do this straight: no diet drugs, whether prescription, over-the-counter, or over-the-Internet. This includes herbs that act like drugs on the body. Take all medication prescribed for your physical and emotional well-being, of course, but don't beg your doctor for diet pills. Establish a precedent for turning within to gather strength rather than depending on a drug that is, if you think of it, not that different from depending on food.

Diet drugs have a less-than-illustrious track record. While many other medications have been around for decades, the diet pills prescribed to me in my teens and twenties are long gone. At that time those were predominantly amphetamines—speed. They were shown to decrease appetite, but when I took them I didn't

144

eat because I couldn't sit still long enough. More recently we've had drugs like fen-phen taken off the market in the 1990s because it was found to cause serious heart damage in some patients.

Presently, your doctor might prescribe a newer, safer appetite suppressant. Unlike the prescription amphetamines of my youth, today's diet drugs won't make you a raving lunatic, but they may not do much to make you thinner either. The problem is you can't stay on them forever. Best-case scenario is that you will learn to eat more reasonably while taking the drugs and keep that up afterward. Results are usually disappointing, probably because the soul and the spirit, where the problem often starts, aren't easily treated with medication.

An alternative munition in your physician's arsenal is a prescription fat blocker. It keeps you from absorbing fat from the foods you eat via its elegant ability to give you diarrhea if you eat a high-fat meal. Of course, any overeater with a talent for manipulation (and let's admit it, that's most of us) can figure out that if you want a cheeseburger, onion rings, and a milk shake, you can skip taking your pill.

Over-the-counter drugs and herbs that promise to curb your appetite, melt fat, or "rev your metabolism" have their own problems. No legitimate studies have shown them to be effective, and aerobic exercise will do all these things free of charge. The ingredients in these products aren't necessarily benign either. Many are some combination of ephedra (*ma huang*), *guaranja*, and caffeine. These are mild central nervous system stimulants (if you missed the sixties, here's your chance), and in moderate amounts for healthy people they are not dangerous. If you have high blood pressure or thyroid disease, or you are prone to anxiety attacks, however, they could spell trouble.

Curiously, *ma huang* and *guaranja* are both respected herbs in the pharmacopeia of traditional Chinese medicine. *Ma huang*, properly prescribed, can be effective in treating asthma. A doctor of traditional Chinese medicine would not prescribe it for weight loss, however. We know about drug abuse. This is herb abuse. Use the strength you have inside you and the power of the God you believe in instead.

With that strength and power, and the help of the other suggestions in this book, you will lose weight without going through the tortures of the damned. You won't need something to ease the pain. You're simply going to be eating the way a normal-sized person eats. At times it will be uncomfortable because that cushion of extra food is gone, but the level of discomfort will be like, let's see, getting your teeth cleaned. This isn't a root canal. I think you can handle it.

60

DEAL WITH YOUR STRESS

There are some quick fixes (hurray!—we like those)

for stress management that aren't half bad.

MANY PEOPLE WITH WEIGHT problems eat to calm down, soothe themselves, and smooth the rough edges off the day. If you learn to do that soothing and smoothing in other ways, you've freed yourself from one reason—reason, not excuse—for using food as a mind-altering substance. Not only will this help you lose weight; it will give you alternatives that work far better than food does.

Food is a pretty pathetic mind-altering substance anyway. Although carbohydrates may have a slight soothing effect, it's minimal. Unlike alcohol or drugs, which actually change your state of mind, food generally functions in this capacity only while you're eating it. Isn't that a rotten break, to go to all the trouble to have an addiction to something that doesn't really *do* anything?

Anyway, this is your opportunity to learn new methods for dealing with life's inevitable imperfections. There are numerous ways to go about this, and some of them are detailed in this book. You might take a stress management course (hospitals, community colleges, and adult ed centers offer them; so do enlightened workplaces). Learning yoga or meditation, getting regular exercise, seeing a qualified counselor or therapist, and looking more closely at what your religion has to offer are all legitimate stress-reduction tactics. So are keeping a journal and talking out problems and decisions with someone who will listen more than talk.

There are even some quick fixes (hurray!—we like those) for stress management that aren't half bad. The easiest and most readily available is breathing. Slow, deep breathing—in through your nose, out through your mouth—can calm you down when you're anxious or angry. A hot bath will work, too, especially if you add a scented destressor like lavender oil. Self-massage—kneading the kinks out of your shoulders, neck, and hands—is pleasant, and getting somebody else to squeeze the tension from your back and trapezius muscles can be a slice of paradise. (Ask somebody to do this for you and offer to do it for him or her.) A change of scene—go outside if you're inside, lie down if you're up, take a walk if you're stewing on the couch—can help; and a good belly laugh will nourish you with a cocktail of calming, healing biochemical reactions.

When you stop using food to deal with stress, you will be discarding a tool that may have served you for a long time. You need to replace it with other tools. Making the switch isn't the easiest thing you'll ever do—change never is—but these stress-defeating devices will eventually perform better for you than food ever did. And they won't hang around on your hips.

61

Shop the Produce Section First

~

The new definition of a balanced diet may be more a palette

of colors than a compendium of chemicals.

Some people are overweight from eating too much food, others from eating too little produce. You know how important fruits and vegetables are. In addition to being low in calories, both are full of vitamins, minerals, and the phytochemicals that researchers say protect against cancer and other degenerative diseases. We need to rediscover produce. It's not "diet food" or "rabbit food." It's food that makes people feel light, healthy, and full of life.

Fruits and vegetables come in rainbow colors for a reason: nature wanted them to attract our attention so we would eat them. The researchers who study disease-preventing phytochemicals suggest that the surest way to get a wide variety of them is to eat produce of different colors. They have found that red tomatoes contain different phytochemicals than blue berries, yellow squash, and green peas. The new definition of a balanced diet may be more a palette of colors than a compendium of chemicals.

While you're in the produce section, think about making, or regularly purchasing from a juice bar, freshly squeezed juice.

Fresh fruit juice is as different from the canned or bottled kind as a live concert is from a car radio. It's sweet, so dilute it by one-third to one-half with pure water. Fresh vegetable juice provides a nutrient infusion. This may be my imagination, but every time I drink it I feel as if my cells are celebrating.

I've found that drinking fresh juice is incompatible with excessive or unwise eating because it is such a strong statement of self-care. In addition, fresh juice has a wild, earthy flavor that is appealing only when you're eating reasonably well. Twinkies and carrot-celery-beet juice just don't work together. Drink at least one glass of freshly extracted juice every day, either with a meal or for a midafternoon pick-me-up. You'll feel healthy, satisfied, and good about yourself.

62

GET COMFORTABLE WITH
YOUR UNCLAD SELF

~

Make friends with your body, part by part if not all at once.

MAKE PEACE WITH YOUR BODY when you're not wearing clothes. I am not suggesting that you vacation at a nudist camp, do your housework in the buff, or sunbathe *au complet*. All I'm saying is that it's your body; come to know and accept how it looks and feels when it's not covered up.

Every so often, some weight loss expert will advise her devotees to stand naked before a full-length mirror and grow more appalled by the minute. The horror of the folds and the bulges is supposed to make Belgian endive more appealing than Belgian waffles. Of course, this kind of mental self-flagellation only erodes what's left of the self-esteem. Instead of this exercise in futility, get comfortable with your unclad self. Don't start by posing in front of a mirror in the full monty. Start by taking a bath or a shower and being nice to your body. Use a cleanser that smells good. Put lotion on your arms and legs and torso.

After you feel at home doing this, graduate to a daily sesame oil massage. Buy sesame oil at a health food store, warm it slightly (put some in a plastic bottle and hold it under a hot tap), and massage yourself before your morning shower. Start with your head and work to your toes. Use long strokes up and down the long bones and round, caressing movements over joints. In India, this self-massage is believed to impart tranquillity and promote healing. It will definitely help you know your body better, and knowing someone is the first step toward loving that person.

Finally, when you're ready, do look at your unclothed body in the mirror. Start with muted light or candles. Describe yourself to yourself with the kindest words you know: strong, curvy, voluptuous, sensual, womanly if you're a woman, masculine if you're a man. Note details about your physical self that you find appealing: the bend of your knee, the reach of your neck, the soft fleshiness of your hands that look as youthful as your daughter's. Make friends with your body, part by part if not all at once. After all, you are in this together.

63

GIVE YOUR SENSES
SOMETHING TO DO

~

Become an epicure of sights, sounds, smells, touch, and taste.

OUR SENSES HELP KEEP us alive and help us appreciate that we are. Those of us who have all five of them in working order are blessed in multiples. When I was binge-eating, though, I was starving in a sensory way, and other people have told me that they experienced similar deprivation. We need to give our senses their due by giving them something to do, something they relish.

Eyes like looking at beauty, color, and the passing parade of life. My favorite writing spot is a coffee bar on the corner of 86th Street and Columbus Avenue in New York City. It has wrap-around windows and a view of everything I love about New York. There's the fruit vendor across with street with his red and yellow umbrella. The fellow who rides by on a unicycle, often talking on his cell phone and occasionally eating his lunch. The dog walkers with six or eight canines in tow, and one in particular who strolls by every morning with a muscular Rottweiler on one leash and a minuscule Chihuahua on the other. My eyes are happy there and I am, too.

Ears like hearing lovely music, lyrical words, and the voices of people their bearer cares about. Skin and nerve endings and the muscles underneath long for touch and stimulation. And the delicate olfactory nerves that detect smells aspire to catalog them and let them carry us back to the best moments of our lives. Just the other day I stopped in a flower shop, and although I was only buying daisies, the floral designer said, "Smell those," and pointed to lush stems of white flowers I didn't recognize. I leaned over, inhaled deeply, and said, "This smells like my grandmother. It must be tuberose."

"It is," the florist confirmed. Even though I had no conscious knowledge of what a tuberose was, that scent and that word commingled in my memory with the woman who was a goddess in my childhood and who always smelled of flowers.

We who have carried extra pounds could never have denied our sense of taste, could we? Ah, yes—and sometimes we've denied this one most of all. Taste is subtle. Gourmets know it doesn't take a lot to upset it. This is why they sometimes clear the palate between courses with a tiny scoop of sorbet. Both overeating on good food and almost any eating of junk food (over-salted, over-sweetened, deep-fried) blunts this delicate mechanism.

While many people who want to lose weight claim to love food, lots of us can't even taste it unless it's covered with condiments. If you think that fresh fruit isn't sweet enough, or that popcorn has to have butter and salt, or that a baked potato has no flavor other than what you put on it, your taste buds need a reeducation. When you can really taste again, simpler food will be delicious and gratifying.

Think of life as, in part, a sensory smorgasbord. Give all your senses something to do. Become an epicure of sights, sounds, smells, touch, *and* taste. Expect more balance and more delight.

64

DEVELOP YOUR MIND
AND YOUR TALENTS

You can't be engrossed in your intellect or your talents and

simultaneously be engaged in an eating spree.

EATING IS A WONDERFUL part of life—*one* wonderful part of life. Watch it take its place in the hierarchy of good things as you focus more on developing your mind and your talents. What did you once love to do that you aren't doing now? Take it up again. What have you always wanted to do that you've never done? Try it. The things you can do, and what you can learn, are fascinating and absorbing. You can't be engrossed in your intellect or your talents and simultaneously be engaged in an eating spree.

Some people have bought the myth that to express their talent as an artist of whatever stripe they need to have some compulsive disorder. They cite the famous writers, musicians, and painters who were alcoholics or in some other way involved with a substance in an ill-advised fashion. If the people who buy this romantic fantasy don't drink to excess, abuse drugs, or have random sexual encounters, overeating will do.

I justified mine after seeing a film about the playwright Lillian Hellman. In one scene she was shown drinking booze from the bottle, chain-smoking, eating a hero sandwich, and *typing all the while*. I was impressed. I figured that if I were to have a shot at becoming a great writer, I had to bear the torment of my painful relationship with food. This was more absurd than the rest of my rationalizations put together. The truth was, I did my best writing when I wasn't under the influence of stuffed pizza. A lot of what I produced while on binges, when I wrote at all, was self-absorbed drivel.

So, artists and others: develop your mind and your talents. And call a spade a spade. If you want to eat half the convenience store, that's your concern, but it has nothing to do with art.

65

BE WARY OF DIETARY FADS
AND FASHIONS

~

You can't fill newspapers, magazines,

and TV airtime with anything indefinitely.

This is why trends enter, peak, and retreat.

WATCH OUT: THERE'S ONE coming. There always is, some dietary fad or trend that captures the media spotlight and convinces people, for a year or two anyway, that it is "the way." Because I am fifty-two years old and was put on diets even as a small child, I have a retrospective view of dieting. I've seen numerous diets go in and out of favor and come round again. My earliest memories are of starches' being considered fattening. (My mother tells how, when she was pregnant with me, the doctor told her she could keep smoking but she'd have to cut out pasta so she wouldn't gain too much weight. Lucky for me, her instincts told her to give up cigarettes, and she did.)

Calorie counting came next. Every morsel went into the calculation. I remember having trouble with the multiplication table in third grade, but I got As in addition; I'd been practicing for years. Then there were the various mono-diets: nothing but grapefruit, nothing but bananas, nothing but hard-boiled eggs. The no-carbohydrate diet first surfaced in the sixties and has come around every five years or so since, like a comet whose appearance astronomers can predict with precision. The original Weight Watchers food plan had me weighing meat and cheese and one daily starchy veg but let me binge on "free vegetables." In fact, that was how I learned to binge: a few cookies used to do it for me; when I was trying to get a food fix on cabbage, it took several heads. (My understanding is that today's Weight Watchers program is excellent, and the organization is to be commended for having a viable philosophy that responds to current knowledge as it develops.)

Fasting was popular in the seventies. Its name fits because it is the fastest way, short of surgery, to lose weight, and it is the fastest way to gain it back and more besides. Then there were the diets named for locations: Beverly Hills I could understand; Scarsdale never sounded that appealing. Food combining (don't mix starch and protein), along with eating only fruit in the morning, was big in the early eighties, just before I gave up the fight. By the time low-fat came into vogue, I wasn't eating a lot of fat anyway. I never entered The Zone, and I've watched no-carb hit it big twice since then.

The point of all this: you'll never keep up. Nobody could. The Absolutely Perfect Diet for All People may be out there. It may even be one of the fads that has come and gone. It doesn't matter. You can't fill newspapers, magazines, and TV airtime with anything indefinitely. This is why trends enter, peak, and retreat. The helpful ones follow the same pattern as the harmful ones. You protect yourself by getting out of the loop.

If you feel a loss when you do this, and you will if diet-tracking has been a longtime avocation, consider the myriad things going on that are important to vast numbers of people, even though you or I may be totally unaware of them. For example, when you were a teenager, you may have followed popular music and known all the performers and their hits. But if you're forty, the Top 40 may mean nothing to you. Your life is no less rich than it was when you were sixteen; you're just interested in different things. You can have interests other than diet fads, too. Do what works for you today. Let the fads come and go. They will anyway, as long as somebody can make a profit from them.

66

GO AHEAD AND
HAVE A BEAUTIFUL FACE

Go ahead and have a pretty face or a handsome one. In fact,

have a flat-out gorgeous face. You're entitled.

"YOU HAVE SUCH A PRETTY FACE"—the classic lament spoken to the poor fat girl. Heard enough times, it can make you stop wanting a pretty face, just so you won't have to listen to that sappy remark one more time. I say, go ahead and have a pretty face or a handsome one. In fact, have a flat-out gorgeous face. You're entitled. And if someone should say, "You have such a pretty face," with that inflection you know is supposed to be followed by "...if only you could lose some weight," just say thank you. Or "Thanks: so do you." Or give them a real start with: "Thanks. I'm really lucky that way. I try not to let it go to my head."

Of course you're more than a pretty face. Your mind and heart and soul mean much more than expressive eyes, terrific hair, and a movie-star smile. Still, take the gifts you've been given and be grateful for all of them. If you feel you're not good-looking, or that you used to be but you're not anymore, work on your thinking. Many a face that was once interesting at best has come to be widely regarded as beautiful or handsome simply because its possessor came to believe this was so and acted on that belief.

It is your right, if you're interested in this sort of thing, not only to have a pretty face but to enjoy having one. Go *au naturel* if you want, or single-handedly raise the stock value of Estée Lauder. It's your call. Either way, don't let anyone stop you from looking as attractive as you can (or as attractive as you feel like looking today), regardless of your weight. You can spiff and polish all you want. In fact, I recommend it. And you can certainly get fit and be healthy. Thin isn't everything. It's coming—"thin" meaning the body size and composition that is right for you. But don't wait until you believe you're thin enough to start seeing yourself as attractive and healthy. You deserve that now.

67

GIVE YOUR WEIGHT LESS CREDENCE

Losing weight will change one condition: the size of your body.

Making your life more like you want it is up to you.

WE'VE TALKED ABOUT getting food in perspective. Now let's get weight and body image in perspective, too. It is true that being overweight can cause problems in life. Obesity is a health hazard. Fat children are made fun of, and fat adults are left out of things. Large people have to look harder to find stylish clothes, and getting through a day can be physically taxing if you're substantially overweight. In spite of all this, thousands of overweight people have rewarding occupations, happy marriages, well-adjusted children, and impeccable reputations. If you don't, don't blame the weight.

There are women with enviable figures and men with dazzling physiques who are alone, work at dead-end jobs, and get little admiration from those around them. Maybe it's the cards they've been dealt, or maybe they made unwise choices in the past that are being played out now. It's the same for you if you're overweight. Overweight is a condition, a state, a situation—one you are right now changing. Losing weight will change one condition: the size of your body. Making your life more like you want it is up to you.

One way to help remember this is to see your body not as yourself but as your vehicle. Your body, as miraculous as it is, is not you, not nearly the totality of you anyhow. It is, rather, the vehicle that enables you to get around. If you start to see it this way, you identify less with a changing physical shell and more with your glorious, underlying self. You can think of this as your soul or spirit, the part that will go on after you die; or you can think of it as that singular blending of your individuality, your gifts, and your love that will outlive you on earth.

The yogis have a mental exercise in which they ask themselves, "Who am I?" over and over until they realize without question that a human being is like an iceberg: what you see isn't the half of it. Try this yourself and see how it helps you give your weight less credence. When you ask yourself, "Who am I?" time and again in a reflective mood, you'll eventually come to respond less and less with weight-related answers like "I'm a fat man" or "I'm a person who gave up the career I wanted because I thought I was too heavy" or "I'm a young woman who binged and vomited my way through college."

When you get even a glimpse of who you really are, you'll be amazed. So will everybody else.

68

BEWARE OF SABOTEURS

~

It is part of prudence to be on the lookout for people and

situations that could sabotage your new way of life.

THERE'S NO REASON to get paranoid: nobody is going to inject you with fat and sugar against your will. Even so, it is part of prudence to be on the lookout for people and situations that could sabotage your new way of life. These include:

• *Eating buddies.* Because most heavy-duty overeating is done in private, we seldom have a sizable coterie of eating cronies the way heavy drinkers have drinking buds. Still, most of us have had a few. These are the people with whom we've so often shared excess or ill-chosen food that it's practically all we know how to do with them. If these people are important in your life, see if you can steer the activities you pursue together in a healthier direction. Remember, however, that you have no power to change another person, and some eating-buddy relationships may have to be phased out altogether.

• *Busybodies.* Some of these people say, "Just a little won't hurt." (Maybe it won't, but whether or not to have it is up to you, not them.) Others say, "Are you sticking to your diet?" (They've got some nerve, don't they?) Particularly confounding are those persons who are liable to make either comment, depending on their mood. Don't be around these people any more than you have to. If you're bound to them by blood or the placement of your office cubicle, come up with a short but potent list of polite yet powerful rebuttals. (And under your breath, you don't even have to be polite.)

• *Relatives and/or their houses.* If your family eats in such a way as to make overweight seem like a dominant genetic trait, or if you grew up in a "food is love" household, being around certain relatives or even being in their houses may incite the kind of eating you'd rather not do. Until you've changed on the inside and you truly want what is good for you—no willpower required— avoid these environments.

If you want to see one of these people, or if you feel an obligation to do so, choose neutral territory: a museum, a café, a matinee. And remember that, with relatives, what they say and what you hear aren't necessarily the same. A comment your dad makes when you're thirty can carry the echo of something he said when you were thirteen. Give your parents and the other people who love you a break: you mean the world to them, after all. But if being around them is a binge trigger, make the necessary arrangements to be a loving son/daughter/sister, etc., and keep out of your mouth any food you haven't consciously chosen to put there.

• *Office parties, baby showers, trick-or-treat.* Look out for yourself. If you have to, schedule a dentist's appointment for party time. Send the baby a gift so special the parents-to-be won't miss you. Give the goblins coins instead of candy. Hear me well: this is not the way you will always have to live. When you're secure in yourself, you can go anywhere you please and sugar up those little kids all you want (although you may no longer want to). For now, don't let yourself be ambushed. Stay on sentry duty.

69

ASSESS YOUR MODERN CONVENIENCES

~

Contemporary life, if we choose to partake of all its

easy-living options, generates overweight.

I READ IN FOURTH or fifth grade—in *My Weekly Reader*, I think—that a secretary who switched from a manual typewriter to an electric one would gain four pounds every year if she didn't make up for the eliminated energy expenditure some other way. That bit of trivia has stayed with me as I've watched life become less and less demanding of physical effort. When I was in elementary school, you had to get up to change the channel and walk to where the phone was (most households had only one). Now everything is as convenient and automatic as possible.

Think about receiving and responding to a letter as opposed to an E-mail. With the letter you have to walk to your mailbox, open and read the communication, go to where you keep stationery and pens, write a response, address and seal the envelope, and take it to a mail drop or the post office. With an E-mail, you read, key in your reply, click "Send," and that's it. No part of your physical being was involved save your fingers and your close-up vision. It's no wonder people are more prone to gaining weight here and now than any other place and time in history.

Assess the modern conveniences in your home and office, as well as how dependent you are on them. The biggies are the job you do—probably not manual labor—and having an automobile that takes you almost everywhere you want to go. Look around you and note others. The point of this is to help you understand one reason why keeping your weight down has been a challenge—through no fault of your own other than taking advantage of what we're told is the best life has to offer. Decide what you want to do about it. Maybe you'd like to make some changes: manual transmission, a can opener that doesn't plug in, walking the stairs at work instead of taking the elevator.

At least you can see why eating a bit more sparingly and including some planned exercise in your life is not retribution, bad luck, or a curse wrought by some genetic propensity to store fat. Contemporary life, if we choose to partake of all its easy-living options, generates overweight. This is simply a fact that you can work with and work around.

70

GET CHECKED OUT PHYSICALLY

It makes sense to know the state of your health

before you set out to improve it.

WHEN I WAS GROWING up, it was common to hear people say, "He's so heavy, it must be glandular." That was later uncovered as more of an excuse than a routine occurrence. Still, it's important to know what is going on with you physically as you embark on lifestyle changes that will alter your physical state. There are medical conditions that can cause weight gain—thyroid and liver disease, for instance. Some medications—steroids of various types, birth control pills, hormone replacement therapy—cause some people to gain weight. Even something as seemingly innocuous as iron pills can stimulate the appetite in certain people.

In addition to conditions and medications that can contribute to weight gain, overweight itself increases the risk for disorders including type II diabetes, heart disease, and stroke. A sedentary person with an undiagnosed heart condition, for instance, could embark on a vigorous exercise program and end up dead. It makes sense, then, to know the state of your health before you set out to improve it. This information may affect how you need to eat or the kinds and amount of exercise that would be right for you.

Besides, the more information you have about yourself—in this case about your health—the more responsibility you can take for your life. You need to know your cholesterol level and your blood pressure, the results of regular breast and gynecological exams if you're a woman, prostate screening results if you're a man, and colon cancer screenings if you're over fifty. Armed with this information, you can make wise decisions about how to live. Almost nobody likes going to the doctor, but do it. Think of it as a safety clearance for losing weight once and for all.

71

LEARN TO WAIT

〜

Once you can wait, you can do almost anything.

EMPTINESS IS SCARY. Overweight people more often eat to fill empty time or uncertainty than to fill empty stomachs. One reason we tend to drive everywhere instead of walking is that walking takes time, empty time; a lot of us don't like that. It's not just heavy people who are skittish about emptiness, though. Look at all the thin ones chewing gum, nursing a soda or a cocktail, or turning on the TV as soon as they walk into the house. Plenty of slim people have to engage in mindless chatter or read a flyer, circular, or trashy tabloid somebody dropped on the bus just so they'll have something to do.

Ours is a culture that detests and fears emptiness, waiting, *being* for its own sake. Nevertheless, you'll have a hard time staying thin for life—or six months for that matter—if you don't learn to wait. I'd be lying if I said it was easy. It may be the toughest suggestion of the 101 you'll find in this book, but it is among the least expendable.

In *Siddhartha*, Hermann Hesse's story of the Buddha, he hammered home the message that all we really need to learn is "to think, to wait, and to fast." While I do not recommend extended fasting for weight loss, if you think of the daily time between meals and the nightly span from dinner to breakfast as fasting, I agree with Hesse completely. Sometimes you just have to wait.

You've had lunch. You feel uncomfortable, and that feels like *hungry*. Wait. You're early to the movie, and you want to buy Milk Duds or bite your nails. For a little while, wait. You hear some juicy gossip you're dying to pass on. Before you do, set aside some time to wait. Just wait. You get angry with someone and want to give that person a piece of your mind. Wait. Peace of mind just might show up.

Having daily quiet time (Chapter 57) will help a lot in training you to "think, wait, and fast." Meditation can be boring. So can the empty spaces in the rest of our lives. Get used to them. Get comfortable participating in them. They can't hurt you. Once you can wait, you can do almost anything. Waiting for weight loss won't be so hard—you already know that only the slow kind lasts. Waiting for good times when life seems dreary will become more tolerable. Waiting for the results of your efforts and for your dreams to come true can get to be downright pleasant.

72

GET PLENTY OF SLEEP

~

Sleepy people tend to be hungry people.

SLEEPY PEOPLE TEND to be hungry people. It makes sense since eating elevates the blood sugar level, resulting in a temporary energy boost. Men and women who are sleep-deprived want that boost even though they need a nap, a few good nights' sleep, or a restful vacation. Sweet cravings are particularly acute in people who have not had enough sleep. These people aren't just looking for just the gradual blood sugar elevation of a balanced meal or healthy snack: they want the straight-to-the-bloodstream rush of a candy bar or a chocolate shake.

Lack of sleep can also be responsible for nervousness and irritability, and a sugar infusion can act as a short-term tranquilizer. People who don't get enough deep sleep can suffer from muscle and joint pain, tender points throughout the body, and seemingly endless fatigue. It's believed that these symptoms are caused by a lack of HGH, human growth hormone, that is secreted during that deepest stage of sleep, when all the muscles are totally relaxed. HGH also plays a role in controlling appetite and burning fat. (This is the same hormone, by the way, that some of the *über-rich* receive by injection because of its purported ability to slow the aging process.)

If you have insomnia and traditional remedies aren't helping, see a sleep specialist. You'll be far more relaxed in your weight loss process if you're sleeping at night. If you don't have insomnia but you're missing out on sleep because you're burning your candle at both ends and in the middle, take stock. Read Chapter 77, "Keep Things Simple," and take steps to cut through the maze of your days to allow for more sleep at night. Sleep needs are on a bell curve: some people need very little, others a great deal, but most of us fall in a midrange of eight to nine hours a night. If you haven't been getting that much, you'll need even more for a while to make up the shortfall. If it seems like a ridiculous waste of time, look at it this way: you can't eat when you're asleep.

Besides, if you're looking to change the way you see yourself, the way you relate to food and to life, and to be open to a spiritual transformation, you need to feel good, think clearly, and avail yourself of all the help you can get. A good night's sleep is one helper you don't want to be without.

73

ALLOW FOR SANE INDULGENCES

This isn't being flighty or selfish or undependable;

it's simply treating yourself as well some of the time

as you treat other people all the time.

THE OLD WEIGHT LOSS style was to reward yourself for staying on a diet, for exercising, for losing five pounds. My dad, distraught that he had a pudgy kid, used to pay me $5 for every five pounds I lost. I made out like a bandit losing the same five pounds over and over until he caught on.

When you eat well, though, your reward is feeling better. When you exercise, your reward is more energy and greater strength. When you lose five pounds, your reward is that you've lost five pounds. Additional rewards are superfluous. What you do need, though, are indulgences. Especially if you formerly indulged yourself only with excessive or unhealthy food, you need to allow for other indulgences and enjoy them without guilt.

Tourists can be delightful examples of people who, for a time at least, know how to indulge themselves. Not long ago I met a charming British couple in their fifties who were visiting New

York. They told me which monuments and museums they'd visited and what shows they'd seen. Then the woman's face lit up and she added, "I went ice-skating at Rockefeller Center *and* in Central Park." I commented that she must be quite an avid skater to take to the ice twice on a seven-day vacation. "Oh, no," she said. "I haven't skated since I was a girl." This woman crossed an ocean, endured jet lag, and spent $300 a night on a hotel room to do something she could have been doing for thirty years.

Don't wait. Act like a tourist. Indulge yourself. Take a day off for your own purposes: maybe a day of beauty at a posh salon or a day in the woods with nothing but your journal and your camera. You can indulge yourself in picking the movie if you're one who always lets your partner or your friends decide. You can from time to time indulge yourself by staying home if you'd like or going out if you'd rather, even if it means changing previously made plans. This isn't being flighty or selfish or undependable; it's simply treating yourself as well some of the time as you treat other people all the time.

You might also buy yourself something you're drawn to, even if you don't really need it—not every day, but when this bauble or that bric-a-brac really speaks to you. When your indulgence costs money, make a pact with yourself that you'll stick with what you can pay cash for. You don't need a debt problem giving you an excuse to overeat.

74

Take Stitches in Time

⌒

Tend to the little rips, tears, and loose buttons of life

before you find yourself in the middle of the street half-dressed

and wondering what happened.

My mother used to tell me, "A stitch in time saves nine." Now, my mom was a liberated woman a good two decades early. She had a career, never learned to sew, and didn't know the first thing about stitches. Still, her mother had recited this adage to her, and they both knew plenty about getting along in the world. Taking that stitch in time is tending to the little rips, tears, and loose buttons of life before you find yourself in the middle of the street half-dressed and wondering what happened.

Welcome to Tailoring 101.

• *Lesson 1: Pay close attention to your internal comfort indicators.* My most obvious and reliable indicator is located, appropriately, in my stomach. When something isn't right, my stomach feels cold, queasy, and—who'd have thought it?—empty. That feeling is a powerful prompt that I need to tend to something, some work I've let slide or a misunderstanding I haven't tried to remedy.

When people talk about eating to numb their feelings, what they're really numbing are the physical indicators that let them know something is amiss. When you no longer do this, you will feel uncomfortable more often, but you can take care of the situation and the resultant discomfort before either gets out of hand.

• *Lesson 2: Get used to doing things now.* Tomorrow may be a great day, but you can't count on tomorrow. Besides, it's far less likely to be a great day if you carry into it incidents that would have been better dealt with today. Procrastination is a big liar. It says, "Wait a while. It will get easier." No, it won't. The only reasons for waiting before tending to something sticky are: if you need more information, if you're upset and might say something you'd later regret, or if it's a situation that's none of your business and you shouldn't be interfering anyway. In that case, procrastinate until politicians get honest. Otherwise, speak now and then forever hold your peace.

• *Lesson 3: If you think you owe an apology, an explanation, or seventy-five cents, you probably do.* Keep your dealings aboveboard and your relationships in good repair. Deal with mistakes and mix-ups early enough that they can be easily taken care of. Otherwise, they get muddied by time, white lies, colorful lies, and other intruders.

Life works better when making restitution, making amends, and making things right as best you can becomes the natural way of things. We're all human, and despite our best intentions, we're going to screw up sometimes. When you're in the restitution habit, your failings won't wreak nearly the havoc that they otherwise might. It's kind of fun actually, figuring out ways to even the score so that, whether the other person heads up your fan club or not, you at least know you've done what you can.

Not long ago I was writing in a coffee shop when my wireless phone rang. I took the call, and although I thought I spoke softly, it annoyed the woman at the next table no end. After I hung up, she reamed me about talking on the phone in a public place. I apologized (she did have a point), but she would have none of it. I was, in her opinion, scum. A few days later I saw her again and offered her my pristine copy of *The New York Times*, saying that since I'd kept her from enjoying her paper the other morning, I'd like her to have mine today. She declined, but she *smiled*. Whether I ever see her again or not, I think we're okay.

Admittedly, it's easier with strangers and casual acquaintances than with the people close to us and those whose opinions of us seem terribly significant. But once you're used to making things right with the easy people, doing it with the more intimidating ones gets simpler. This is not bowing and scraping. It's becoming a bigger human being.

THINK AND SPEAK POSITIVELY

Get so many of your hopes up that half of them could come

to naught and you'd still come out ahead.

YOU DON'T HAVE TO become Pollyanna, but it wouldn't hurt to rent the movie. Your body, your life, and your world are all paying attention to the thoughts you think and the words you speak. These are the raw materials they build on. Say "I'm hopeless" often enough and you lose hope. Think "I can do this" with sufficient conviction and you'll prove yourself right.

Do not expect to overhaul your attitude overnight. Left to my own devices, I would fall into a spontaneous pessimism. Whether I was born with this ability or learned it, I am possessed of a propensity for seeing every possible way things could go wrong. I still have to work sometimes at putting a sunny spin on the events of my life or envisioning a positive outcome to some particular event. I have improved quite a bit. Otherwise I'd probably be fat again. I mean, why not? If life is that dismal, you're at least entitled to a couple quarts of rocky road. Daily.

I have found that the most effective means for lifting my genetically glum disposition is to speak positively. I may be thinking,

"This won't work. This can't work. And you're crazy if you think it's got a chance in hell." But instead I can say, "That sounds good. Let's give it a shot." This isn't lying. If I had logical reasons for believing why whatever it is couldn't fly, I would certainly voice them. More often than not, though, I'm just figuring something awful will happen because somewhere along the line I decided it was dangerous to get my hopes up.

Get them up! Way up! Get so many of your hopes up that half of them could come to naught and you'd still come out ahead. Speak positively first. Your thoughts will follow suit.

Eschew Fast Food

⌒

Regard it in the spirit of the Donner party:

on rare occasions you have to eat something you never

would under ordinary circumstances.

You are an adult, and you have every right to make your own decisions about what you eat. Since you are probably an adult who has dieted many times and studied nutrition as thoroughly as any layperson might, I can only make suggestions to you as someone who has been blessed with something you want, too. Therefore, I strongly suggest that you eschew fast food. Avoid it. Stay away from it. Regard it as unfit for someone of your stature and worth (it is). It is the sustenance of last resort, to be regarded in the spirit of the Donner party: on rare occasions you have to eat something you never would under ordinary circumstances.

There are two primary reasons for giving the golden arches and their compatriots wide berth. One is obvious: it can be easily argued that the food is of inferior quality, both as cuisine and as nutrition. For the most part it is greasy, salty, low in fiber, and high in calories. Just about the only people who can frequent fast-food places without gaining weight are active children and teenagers, and even these age groups are, statistically, fatter than they've ever been. And this food is often processed to *Brave New World* proportions. Most of it was shipped in from far away, frozen or dehydrated. It may have once been a cow grazing on the prairie or a potato rooted in Idaho soil, but heaven only knows how long ago that was. With a few exceptions, such as the Subway chain, providing fresh, healthful food is not a high value in the fast-food industry.

The other reason you don't need this particular kind of break today is more subtle—and more insidious. Fast food, because it is ubiquitous and cheap, is diminishing the quality of life in America and around the world. It seems hell-bent on eliminating dining as an *experience*. It has infected agriculture, once a sacred pact between humans and the land, with an attitude of alienation, in which neither the land nor the livestock nor the eventual consumer has value beyond economics. A fast-food lifestyle is creating bodies we don't want for ourselves and a world we don't want for our children. Drive past instead of "thru." Cook. Pack a lunch. Go to an ethnic café, an elegant restaurant, or even a congenial diner. Swear off eating at any place where parking is optional.

If you have absolutely no choice other than a fast-food meal, make the best selection from the meager ones available (see Chapter 58, "Make the Best Possible Choices from Those Available"). When I'm in this situation—usually driving on an interstate—I might get a bean burrito at Taco Bell or a salad and baked potato at Wendy's. It's not haute cuisine, but it passes as food, and in a pinch it will do.

77

KEEP THINGS SIMPLE

⌒

Overwhelmed *and* overeat

have more in common than a prefix.

LOSING WEIGHT AND keeping it off is not an occupation, and you don't have to resign from your life to do it. Nevertheless, you are attempting to accomplish something at which 98 percent of people fail. This is a major operation. If you were going to climb Mount Everest or sail across the Atlantic in a skiff, you would clear off your calendar months in advance to train, plan, and prepare. You've embarked on something equally momentous. Cut yourself some slack by keeping your food choices simple, your schedule streamlined, your possessions manageable, and your affairs in order.

Look first at your level of busyness. To an extent, staying busy is helpful. It can engage you in the world and with the other people who inhabit it. It will keep your mind from obsessing over food and over whether or not your triceps jiggle. For some people, though, being occupied itself becomes an obsession. If you're busy, you must be important, right? People are counting on you, and what you do matters. This may be, but cutting down on appointments and obligations may be just what you need to give yourself time to focus on the business at hand.

Besides, *overwhelmed* and *overeat* have more in common than a prefix. When you're committed to more than you can realistically do, you're unlikely to take the time to eat well and enjoy your meals. Exercise will get short shrift, and it's unlikely that you'll have the energy or the inclination to work at a new way of living that will keep you in a body you'll be proud of for years to come.

Possessions can complicate your life, too, if you have too many of them. Their acquisition and upkeep can interfere with the care you owe yourself and the attention you want to give the people and projects that mean something to you. The amount of paraphernalia people need to own or have around them varies from person to person. An inordinately high percentage of men and women with weight problems, however, have clutter problems, too. It seems that we like hanging on to things—clothes that don't fit, textbooks from college, the last ten pounds.

Letting go of the excess can be hard—horrifying even—for certain people, so take it slow and easy. In recent years the ultimatum to get organized has been high on the cultural "should" list—right up there with losing weight. This isn't about organization, though. It's about clearing space, literally and figuratively, so there's room for more delight in your life. Don't worry for a long, long time about cleaning out messy drawers that you seldom open anyway. Just be aware of any excess that bothers you. Start with what's old, stale, and not useful to you today. If it's of use to somebody else, pass it on. If it's recyclable, recycle it. Just get it out, let it go.

Then assess the complexity level of your life as a whole. How much of your time is going toward what really matters to you, and how much of it is tied up with technicalities, miscellany, and putting out fires that you yourself may have had a hand in starting? Don't skip over this one: a lot of people with food problems find excitement (positive or negative), suspense, and intrigue as attractive as any dessert tray. Leave drama for the stage and screen. Avoid the entanglements that get people in no end of trouble—living on the edge, taking on unsecured debt, dating someone that all your friends and your gut instincts have warned you against. If you are increasing your spiritual awareness, investing yourself in good work, and involving yourself with good people, there will be plenty of excitement in your life. You won't have to look for it in chancy places.

78

SAMPLE ETHNIC CUISINES

⌒

The typical American diet is pretty boring without

some help from the rest of the planet.

THE WORLD IS FULL of marvelous things, and some of those things you can eat. One reason for overindulging is getting into a rut with the same old food. The typical American diet is pretty boring without some help from the rest of the planet. You can expand your dietary horizons without expanding your waistline by exploring culinary offerings from around the globe.

In many countries vegetables figure more prominently in entrées than they do here. Most native cuisines are built around a basic starch—rice, pasta, kasha, corn, taro, or dark wheat or rye bread—and other foods round out the diet. Don't let the word *starch* frighten you. It hasn't made the Chinese fat, and it won't make you fat either if you're refraining from junk food, choosing whole instead of refined carbohydrates when they're available, and eating reasonable portions of everything else.

You can tour the world in your own hometown by sampling the cuisines offered there. Saigon 39 is a charming Vietnamese restaurant in my neighborhood in Kansas City. It's owned by a perennially youthful woman named Mimi who credits much of her success to blessings from the Buddha, a statue of whom enjoys shrine space near the cash register. In keeping with the tenets of Mahayana Buddhism, Mimi and her staff place food offerings on the altar every morning. Evidently not all their customers understood the custom, because Mimi had to put up a sign that said, "You may rub the Buddha's tummy for luck, but please don't eat his offerings." I don't know about you, but I find it captivating to go to a restaurant where I can get a comparative religions lesson along with the spring rolls.

Go to Vietnamese restaurants—and Italian, Indian, Thai, Korean, Ethiopian, Middle Eastern, and other kinds of restaurants, too. If you live where there isn't a lot of ethnic diversity, make a point of sampling the cuisines of the world when you travel to other places. Experience flavors your taste buds have waited for all your life. Go with friends so you can order several dishes and share. Eat slowly and savor new aromas, tastes, and textures. Relax. Relish. Study the artifacts that decorate the tables and the walls. Ponder the fascinating juxtapositions of art, culture, religion, and food. Listen to music that may sound strange played on instruments you may have never heard before. Have a nice evening. Leave a nice tip.

79

CREATE AMENABLE CIRCUMSTANCES

Build amenable circumstances carefully,

the way a proud mason lays each brick.

YOUR LIFE DOES NOT have to be fantastic all the time for you to lose weight and not gain it back. Still, you're entitled to the best possible life you can get. Having amenable circumstances means that you like your life. This is big. Ideally, agreeable circumstances provide you with the elements conducive to happiness—satisfying work, a supportive relationship, a comfortable home, and the like. These do not guarantee happiness, since that is an internal stance not entirely dependent on external conditions. Nevertheless, all human beings strive for life circumstances that suit them. The particulars vary from person to person.

Creating amenable circumstances can take time, probably more time than it will take for you to release your extra weight. A frenzied quest for amenable circumstances *yesterday* causes people to make impulsive moves. They might buy new furniture, find new careers, even look for new spouses or take lovers on the side. This isn't the way to do it. You need to build amenable circumstances carefully, the way a proud mason lays each brick, knowing that the structure he is building will outlast his own life.

Start slowly. Look at your environment, your daily routine, the various roles you play. What can you do to create somewhat more amenable circumstances in one of these areas? Do that. Live with the change for a while. See how it suits you. Then move on to the next thing.

In one sense, your life itself is a creative process so enormous it makes painting the Sistine Chapel ceiling look like a craft project. Take it on by creating the circumstances that make you smile and let you shine.

80

LAUGH AND PLAY

Play is a vacation from the earnestness of life.

LAUGH AND PLAY. Have some fun. Engage often and intensely in merriment, gaiety, and frolic. Be silly. Go to humorous movies. Download jokes, and if one is really funny, laugh uproariously. You're doing yourself a favor. Laughter floods your system with all kinds of fabulous chemicals that make you feel content and complete—a pretty good replication of "full."

Well-adjusted children have great respect for recreation and overlook no opportunities to play. I learned as a home-schooling mother that play is also the premier tool in the educational storehouse. What children learn through play stays with them, not just for the quiz but for the duration. Whatever your age, play is a vacation from the earnestness of life. It does for your brain what defragmenting does for your computer: you can't work while either is going on, but when you come back you find things cleaned up, cleared out, and back in order.

When I was overeating, I couldn't play worth a darn. Even after my eating was on track, I suffered from a kind of posttraumatic play disorder. When my daughter was five or six, I actually took a course called "Play for Adults" so I could be a better mom and a more childlike grown-up. I learned there to start slowly, avoid highly competitive sports and games, and watch out for value judgments that give work—any work, all work, and over-work—a status superior to play.

You can also become more playful by doing what you like to do and not apologizing for it. For example, I read *People* magazine when I fly. I used to feel that because I was a writer—a *self-improvement* writer, for goodness sake—I should be reading something that would improve me: *War and Peace* or at least the *The Atlantic Monthly*. And now that half my fellow passengers are hunched over laptops from Detroit to San Francisco, the subliminal message is stronger still: "You ought to be working all the time." But if you can't do escape reading at thirty thousand feet, what kind of world is this? I may not be out playing touch football à la Hyannis Port, but every now and then I can at least read something that requires no effort—and even look at the pictures.

Play is part of the balance piece that will help keep your eating in line without undue distress on your part. It tells the universe it can pass the "woe is me" role on to another actor. You've played that part. It's time for a little comedy.

81

TAKE VITAMINS

Taking a daily supplement may help reduce your cravings

because you're meeting more of your nutrient needs.

THE CONTROVERSY has gone on as long as I can remember: whether we ought to get our nutrients from the food we eat or take supplements to make up any shortfall. The most ardent pro-supplement advocate would allow that someone eating a carefully selected, organically grown, whole-foods diet could get enough vitamins and minerals; and the staunchest foe of supplementation would admit that most people don't eat this way. Even those of us who want to and who give it our best effort rarely do it 100 percent, since we all take road trips and accept dinner invitations and sometimes come home tired and cut corners.

Also, because much of our food is grown on depleted soil and has been processed or shipped over long distances, it has become increasingly difficult to derive ample nutrients from the foods we eat. So take a supplement—at the very least a comprehensive multivitamin/mineral combination suitable for someone of your age and gender. You don't have to buy it at a health food store or spend a lot of money. The Center for Science in the Public Interest compared dozens of multivitamins and found that among the best on the market was plain old Centrum from the drugstore.

What you're looking for is a multi that has a balance of B-complex vitamins, plenty of vitamin C, trace minerals (like zinc and selenium), and antioxidants like vitamin E and beta-carotene. A trace mineral that may be particularly helpful in weight control is chromium, which has been shown to help insulin metabolize sugar more effectively.

Antioxidants are important in keeping down the number of molecular pests called *free radicals*. These result from oxidation and damage your cells the way rust damages your car. It takes thousands of chemical reactions to take a protein molecule and turn it into a cell wall or to take a glucose molecule and turn it into energy; free radicals impede these reactions.

If you want to take more than a multivitamin, educate yourself on the subject or consult a nutritionist or nutritionally aware physician. Certain supplements seem to make some people feel hungrier. I've found that with iron. If you're a man or a post-menopausal woman, a normal diet is more likely to give you too much iron than not enough. Check with your doctor. There's no use taking something you don't need.

Generally speaking, though, taking a daily supplement may help reduce your cravings because you're meeting more of your nutrient needs. Besides, it's one more way to take care of yourself.

82

LEAVE SOMETHING ON YOUR PLATE

⌒

Overeaters are usually charter members of

the clean-plate club. Resign.

PEOPLE WHO DON'T overeat invariably leave food on their plates. When they feel full, they stop eating. If a particular dish doesn't taste good or loses its appeal halfway through, they don't eat any more of it. If they don't like the dish much, they eat just enough to assuage their hunger and leave the rest. Overeaters are usually charter members of the clean-plate club. Resign. Leave something on your plate. At first it will seem contrived—for that matter, it *will* be contrived—but eventually you'll find yourself a far more discriminating diner.

The inability to throw away food is a characteristic of some people with weight problems. I used to have it something awful— you know, the old "people are starving, so I'd better eat it" nonsense. Yes, people are starving. Send a donation. Say a prayer. And leave something on your plate to remind yourself how lucky you are.

It may be a while before you can leave food on your plate without experiencing anxiety about it. Don't rush yourself. Leave a little bit of something when you can. The more often you do this, with trust in a supportive universe and pride in your spectacular self, the more you will realize things have become possible that you never believed could be.

83

Understand Your Rhythms

⌒

Rhythms and cycles affect our moods and our behavior, whether

in something as monumental as the desire for a child or in

something as incidental as the desire for a Popsicle.

PHYSICALLY AND emotionally, we are rhythmic beings governed by cycles and seasons and shifts that affect us through the day, the month, and our lifetime. Our eating behaviors and certain fluctuations in the way our bodies look and feel depend on these rhythms. When you understand yours, and how what is going on around you affects them, you will have an easier time living with equanimity and eating with discretion.

The most obvious cyclic influence in women's lives is the menstrual cycle, keyed to the phases of the moon as surely as the ocean's tides are. If you are a woman in your reproductive years, observe the way your cycle affects your appetite, the foods you're attracted to, the amount of sleep you require, your mood, and your personality. Women who pay close attention often find that, left to their own devices, they would be quieter and more inner-directed during their periods and more assertive and gregarious around the time of ovulation.

Many notice that during the more introverted phase of their cycle they want to eat more carbohydrates and comfort foods—soup, hot cocoa, mashed potatoes like Grandma used to make—while during their watch-out-world weeks they want more salad, protein, iced tea. This alone could be behind the demise of many a diet: if you're trying to eat all the time what your body needs part of the time, it won't work for long. You have to pay attention to yourself (see Chapter 89, "Listen to Your Body") and the patterns of your life.

In addition to the menstrual cycle, all of us are subject to rhythmic forces. According to Ayurvedic philosophy, the day has rhythms: a wake-up energy in the morning that peaks from 5:00 to 7:30, a sleep-inducing energy from 9:00 to 11:00 at night. Western medicine has long documented the physiological cycles that govern processes such as the secretion of hormones. Cortisol levels, for example, are lowest in the middle of the night. They start to rise about 4:00 A.M. and crest around 8:00 A.M., helping energize us for the day.

The emotional phases that characterize our lives are as obvious to the careful observer as the daily cycles that affect our bodies are to the scientist. Many of us know people who were married to their work, obsessed with it even, who reached a point when it didn't fulfill them anymore and retirement became mandatory—not because their company demanded it but because their souls did. We have also known people—or maybe *were* people—who had no interest in being parents until one fateful day when all of a sudden nothing else mattered, and having a baby became the most momentous issue in the history of the world.

Rhythms and cycles affect our moods and our behavior, whether in something as monumental as the desire for a child or in something as incidental as the desire for a Popsicle. Use your journal to note what you notice about your own rhythms. When are you hungriest? When are you inclined to exercise, and when are you liable to wimp out? Do naps refresh you or leave you disoriented? (The closest I get these days to the old have-to-eat-no-matter-what urge is when I wake up from a nap. It's as if part of my consciousness stays asleep and a stiff snack might wake it up. Needless to say, I sleep at night and don't nap much.)

Note, too, how weather patterns and seasonal cycles affect your own. If the dead of winter makes you feel dead, too, you may need to plan your vacation for February instead of July, even if it means pulling the kids out of school for a week. Or you may benefit from a special lamp that simulates the spectrum of natural sunlight and helps people who feel depressed in winter make it through with less distress. Knowing your rhythms is one more way to know yourself. The more you do, the easier life gets.

84

GET USED TO SWEATING

~

Sweating is the outward and visible sign of an inward

and health-promoting act.

MY FIRST CONSCIOUS memory of an aversion to sweat was in ballet class. I was six. We were rehearsing for our recital, and all the little girls were wearing yellow satin costumes with glitter and bizarre, Las Vegas–style headdresses. We were supposed to be a flock of chickens. The skinny girls seemed to leap and pirouette without so much as a glow. I was sweating like a field hand. I wasn't dumb. I knew that if I didn't exercise I wouldn't sweat. That was the end of my dance career and, for a long, long time, almost any other exertion I wasn't forced to perform.

Nevertheless, sweating is the outward and visible sign of an inward and health-promoting act. When you sweat from activity (not because it's ninety degrees with 90 percent humidity), you know you're engaging in aerobic activity, the slow burn that uses oxygen, burns fat, tunes up your metabolism, and convinces your cardiovascular system that there might be hope after all.

Years ago for a magazine article, I interviewed Dr. Kenneth Cooper, the cardiologist who coined the term *aerobic exercise*. I remember his saying, "All exercise is good, but only one kind will save your life." That's the aerobic kind, the kind that usually produces sweat.

We've talked about walking. Walking is aerobic if you do it at a steady clip. You could also ride a bike, take classes at the gym, or go swimming (you won't notice the sweat so much, and if you're willing to wear a bathing suit, you're already ahead of the game). The point is to do something that puts enough stress on your respiratory apparatus that you breathe a little heavily but not so much that you can't sustain the activity for twenty minutes or so. While you need to keep it up this long to improve your cardiovascular endurance, you can get the firming, fat-burning, and energizing benefits in shorter spurts too.

New research suggests that, in addition to burning calories and revving metabolism, perspiration-prompting exercise may actually control the appetite. It appears to heighten the effect of a brain chemical called *dopamine*, which produces sensations of satisfaction.

Knowing all this, I must admit that I am still not fond of sweating. In fact, I dislike it about as much as filling out income tax forms or standing in line at the Department of Motor Vehicles. But I'm used to it. About three times a week I make sure I sweat. I do not look forward to it, but it's great when it's over. There are people, even some who start out substantially overweight, who grow to love vigorous exercise. It's their therapy, a social outlet, recreation. They're the ones who take a kick-boxing class and then walk the track "just for fun." I'm the one in the shower immediately after class, erasing the sweat and convinced I've served my time. The jocks and I both get firmer thighs and happier brain chemicals. If they're firmer than I am, good for them. I know they're no happier.

85

KEEP YOURSELF COMFORTABLE

When it is not necessary to undergo discomfort for some

greater good, keep yourself comfortable,

both physically and emotionally.

DISCOMFORT IS A PART of life. We've just been through sweating as a case in point. Waiting for a meal when you'd rather eat now can cause discomfort. So can holding your tongue, giving up something you want for the benefit of another person, and getting through the proverbial helluva time without doing something stupid. Even so, when it is not necessary to undergo discomfort for some greater good, keep yourself comfortable, both physically and emotionally.

Twelve-step programs use the acronym *HALT*: "Don't get too hungry, too angry, too lonely, or too tired." These discomforts, once they reach a certain point, can push a susceptible person to his or her drug of choice. (Yes, cheesecake can count as a drug, depending on how you eat it and what you're thinking when you do.)

Basically, keeping yourself reasonably comfortable is as simple as using heating, air-conditioning, and cross-ventilation to your advantage. It's wearing enough clothes to stay warm in the winter and taking off enough to keep cool in the summer. (I realize you may not want people to see your arms. Believe me, they've seen worse. If it's such a problem that six months of the year you're sacrificing comfort in favor of sleeves, lift weights. Within two weeks, you'll feel a great deal better about your arms.)

Wear clothes that fit and don't chafe or bind. An "I feel fat" mind-set is often the result of wearing clothes or undergarments that are too small. Wear comfortable shoes (*comfortable* needn't mean "dowdy"). Get some comfortable furniture—at least an ergonomically designed office chair if you sit at a desk all day.

If you're seriously overweight, you know that this can be uncomfortable in and of itself. You don't deserve this discomfort, but you will have to put up with it for a while. This is all the more reason to make yourself feel good with long baths, foot rubs, shoulder rubs. Have lovely scents on your body and around your house. Even when you're doing chores, use soft cloths and good sponges and cleaning products that smell nice and don't give you a headache. Surround yourself with art and objects that make you feel good whenever you look at them. You know the phrase "a sight for sore eyes"? Have plenty such sights around your home and office. When they no longer cheer you, put them away. Pull out something you haven't seen in a while.

Keep yourself emotionally comfortable, too. Talk about your problems with a counselor or an understanding friend. Write in your journal. Take walks with yourself or your dog and expect inspiration. Attend to little things before they get bigger. Of course you'll have problems, but seek to have fewer of your own making.

86

Pay Attention to
Your Personal Superstitions

Your superstitions largely determine the state

you're in today. You need to deal with them astutely,

almost like defusing a bomb.

WE ALL HAVE SUPERSTITIONS, beliefs that aren't based on logic but that we hold dear nonetheless. For example, when I was nineteen, I lost weight with a popular diet program and then went to work for the organization. At that time their food plan required everyone to eat fish five times a week. Although it wasn't written anywhere official, there was the widespread belief that all that fish had some supernatural fat-zapping property. I kept close track to be sure I ate enough fish—six or seven or eight times a week when I could. (It takes a committed food addict to eat tuna on toast for breakfast, but I was up for it.)

After some time and soul-searching, however, I decided that I wanted to become a vegetarian. I was scared to death about it, because I *knew* that if I stopped eating fish five times a week I would gain back all my weight and more. It was inevitable. With great trepidation, I did it anyway, and sure enough, I gained back all the weight. And more. Even though most people who become vegetarians lose weight, I got heavier than I'd ever been. I'd known it would happen.

In retrospect, I see that I created a self-fulfilling prophecy. When I stopped eating meat and fish, I started eating with wild abandon. I didn't gain weight because of a fish deficiency but because I was determined, unconsciously of course, to prove my theory right. (I was also just plumb sick of being on a diet. It had been eighteen months—that's as long as being pregnant twice. I was ready to break out.)

Think about what superstitions you hold dear. Do you believe the consequences of a missed workout are so dire that you exercise if you're ill or if you really ought to be doing something else? Do you believe that long-term weight loss is impossible for you because you've always been fat or you come from a fat family? Do you think you can lose weight only if you smoke or take diet pills, because that's the only way you've done it before? Are you so terrified of carbohydrates that you put whole grains, hearty vegetables, and fruit in the same category as refined sugar and white flour?

Your superstitions largely determine the state you're in today. You need to deal with them astutely, almost like defusing a bomb. Quick moves could be dangerous. First, you have to look at each superstition in the bright light of reason. Discuss it with someone you trust. You might run food superstitions past a nutritionist or talk with a counselor about superstitions of the "Other people can do this but not me" sort. Figure out, if you can, where this belief came from. Did someone present it to you? Why do you value that person's opinion so much? Or is the superstition based on your own experience? Is there another possible explanation for what happened to you that caused a superstition to arise from it?

If your superstition is harmless ("I lose weight best when I run on Mondays and Fridays and swim on Tuesdays and Thursdays"), keep it. Considering everything else you're dealing with, you don't need to burden yourself with dismantling a mind-set that isn't causing any trouble. If, on the other hand, your superstition undermines your progress ("There's no way I can lose weight until I can leave this job/this guy/this town"), jeopardizes your health ("I can eat only protein—nothing else"), or just makes you a little bit nutty ("Anything I eat on the weekend doesn't count"), give it up.

VISIT AN ART MUSEUM

~

To have the viable option of being thin, you need to embrace

the concept that fat people can be beautiful, too.

VISIT AN ART MUSEUM with the intention that you are going to look at the nudes. Most of them are voluptuous, even fat by today's standards. They are also beautiful. To have the viable option of being thin, you need to embrace the concept that fat people can be beautiful, too. Doing so does not mean that you will get fat, stay fat, or become fat again. It means that you no longer have to *fear* getting fat, staying fat, or becoming fat again, because you've eliminated the horror of it.

Fear draws to us what we most want to avoid. Combine it with self-loathing and you set up a magnetic attraction that virtually guarantees that what you want least will plague you well into the future. For this reason you must get over thinking that adipose tissue is ugly and grotesque. You need to see folds of flesh the way an artist does. You need to become neutral about fat.

While you're at it, become realistic about bodies. As was touched on in Chapter 16, we are subject to a televised, printed, filmed, and Internetted bombardment of images of models. And models who've become actresses. And women with models' bodies reading the news, playing political pundit, and predicting the weather.

Because these images are literally in your face, it is no easy task to remember that the average American female is 5′4″ tall and weighs 144 pounds. True, 144 pounds is too much weight for many 5′4″ frames, but put this in perspective. Women in this category are not routinely keeling over from premature strokes and heart attacks. They are not unable to attract mates and propagate the species. And when they reach midlife, they often have an easier time with the physiological changes of menopause than their slimmer counterparts.

There is nothing wrong with wanting to lose some weight. It is my intention in writing this book to help you do that once, for all, and forever. But until you do—and after you've done it—you've got to enlarge your concept of attractiveness to embrace large women and portly men.

Get thee to an art museum! You might also consider investing in a coffee-table art book like Gowing's *Paintings in the Louvre*. Reproduced on its cover is *The Valpinçon Bather*, by Jean-Auguste-Dominique Ingres. The subject is a female nude who, if she were alive today, would wear a size eighteen—and that's if she bought expensive clothes. But she's gorgeous. And she's on the cover of a great big, classy book. Put her on your coffee table next to the magazines. Let her give those gaunt women some competition. Glance at her from time to time while you're watching TV to remind yourself that waiflike is not the only appealing look there is.

And branch out with your artistic explorations. It wasn't just in the olden days that artists painted and sculpted bodies of size and stature. In the art of body casting a mold is made of an actual person's torso. It can then be painted and exhibited. For a price you can have a body casting done of yourself, turning your body—today's version of it no less—into art. Of course, it already was. You just have to believe it.

88

Take a Look at Other Imbalances

You can't be choosy about which monkeys you get off your back.

It has to be all monkeys, one at a time perhaps,

but all of them nonetheless.

WHEN YOU ARE CONSISTENTLY eating in a moderate fashion and your body is at a healthy, comfortable place, the mental focus you may have given to food and weight will shift to other imbalances in your life. Don't be caught unawares. Look at your other imbalances before they show up unannounced.

If you smoke, for instance, you are committing suicide the slow way and you know it. Most people can't deal with dropping two well-entrenched habits at once. If you have a choice, quit smoking before you quit overeating since smoking is the more deadly of the two. But if you lose weight and you still smoke, it is incumbent upon you to deal with that next. Yes, it is unfair that some people have no compulsions to overcome and you've got two. But if you want to have a life that is long and rich and full, you can't be choosy about which monkeys you get off your back. It has to be all monkeys, one at a time perhaps, but all of them nonetheless.

There are numerous areas of imbalance that can decrease your quality of life and eventually lead back to overeating. This is because memories of the comfort you once derived from excess food can trick you into believing that using food again can heal the pain wrought by these other excesses. Drugs (including diet pills) might be a problem. So can debt and extravagant shopping or their flip side, monetary deprivation, sometimes referred to as "anorexic spending." A close relationship that's unhealthy can throw off all the balance in your life. So can sex when, like certain foods, it fuels the appetite instead of satisfying it. Overwork is an unbalancer. So is taking on everybody else's problems as your own.

If seeing any of these implicated as a problem area makes you slightly uncomfortable, that may be an area of imbalance for you. Look at it. See how it's affecting your life. If you don't like what you see, see what you can do about it. Slowly. With care for yourself and respect for your (imperfect) humanity. But do deal with it. When some seemingly unrelated imbalance goes too far, you can end up back in the food again and not even realize how you got there.

89

LISTEN TO YOUR BODY

You give yourself a huge advantage by joining forces with your

physiology instead of trying to work against it.

"LISTEN TO YOUR BODY" is an aging adage spawned in the era of "Go with the flow" and "Make love, not war." It isn't trendy, but it is true: your body knows what it needs and will communicate this to you. The old assumption that overweight people have damaged their "appestats" and lost this body wisdom is simply not true. Like everybody else, we can know when we've had enough. We have simply ignored the "enough" signal so long and so successfully that eventually we don't hear it anymore—the way people adjust to living near railroad crossings and firehouses. In reality, though, the body—your body—will not only tell you when you've had enough, it will tell you what it needs to nourish itself *if you listen.*

You may have read the studies showing that small children, when allowed to choose from an array of foods, instinctively consume balanced diets. We still have this innate ability, as long as the array of foods we're choosing from is of high quality.

Start out with a month or two of eating predominantly whole foods—that is, food from nature, minimally refined or tampered with. And be sure you haven't been undereating and making yourself hungry. With this background established, you will be able to go to a grocery store or a salad bar and let your body choose what will go in your cart or on your plate. These will be subtle impulses; listen carefully. Your mind might be saying "macaroni and cheese" while your body is saying "Caesar salad, carrot-ginger soup, brown bread." When you make a point of listening, you'll be able to discern the difference.

Sometimes you'll choose to go with your emotional wants instead of your physical needs. This is allowed. Just acknowledge that you know the difference. Say to your body, "Thanks for the information. This time I'm going to do something else just because I want to, but please keep giving me the messages."

Pay attention to your physical and emotional responses to certain foods and eating situations. It helps to write these observations in your journal. Some discoveries I have made about myself over the years include: it doesn't take much caffeine to make me jittery; it doesn't take much wine to make me sleepy; and if I don't get enough vegetables, I have a greenery alert—a strong yen for spinach salad or sautéed broccoli. Responding to that brings me back into balance.

By listening to your body and honoring its responses, you become more independent, more able to sift through suggestions from others and take only the ones that work for you. For example, a common piece of advice given to dieters is to fortify a fruit snack with a few nuts or a piece of cheese to make the snack more substantive and to slow down the rate at which the body metabolizes the sugar in the fruit. The logic holds up on paper but not necessarily in practice. Nuts and cheese are both high in fat, and salted nuts and most cheeses also pack a lot of sodium, making them prime munchables of the betcha-can't-eat-just-one variety. If in listening to your body and noting your past experience you find that nuts and cheese aren't legitimate snack foods for you, take heed and reserve them for mealtime.

You give yourself a huge advantage by joining forces with your physiology instead of trying to work against it. I don't take this as far as believing that we are all so unique we have to scrap what little is left of the family dinner so each individual can have his or her special meal. Still, paying attention to what works for you and what doesn't only makes sense. Listen to your body. The better the communication between you and it, the better equipped you will be to make sensible choices.

MEET THE NEW FOUR FOOD GROUPS

⌒

Simple foods from nature have formed the foundation of human diets on most of this planet for millennia.

YOU CAN DO WHAT I'VE done without eating the way I eat. Food choices are personal, and yours are none of my business. I would feel that I was withholding information, however, if I did not share mine with you. They are part of the reason that I am able to eat well, be healthy, stay thin, and honestly never feel deprived.

I am a vegetarian, and for the most part I eat vegetables, fruits, beans, soy products, and grains, whole when I can get them. This translates from "foodstuffs" into "cuisine" as veggie burgers and bean burritos; pasta with spring vegetables and sautéed garlic and my mom's marinara sauce; hearty soups (lentil, noodle, vegetable, split pea) and colorful salads with garbanzos and sunflower seeds; sautéed veggies (steamed and roasted, too) topping a baked potato or a whole-wheat roll; black beans and rice; chili and corn bread; and exotic specialties from around the world (see Chapter 78).

The Physicians Committee for Responsible Medicine calls unrefined grains, vegetables, fruits, and legumes the "New Four Food Groups." These are simple foods from nature that have formed the foundation of human diets on most of this planet for millennia. They are foods that the cells of the body understand and know how to deal with in an efficient and health-promoting manner.

I personally don't add animal foods to the equation, but some people successfully do that by keeping the New Four Food Groups as the basis of their meals and using meats, eggs, and dairy products for flavor and interest. Eating this way is highly satisfying and packs such a nutritional punch that every calorie carries its weight. You might have chicken with your rice and veggies, and I might have tofu. Although the vegetarian in me would love to make a case for your choosing tofu, too (I actually do that in my book *Love Yourself Thin*), I would rather see you free and happy than make a case.

There are lots of ideas about diet and nutrition, trends that come and go, and findings that contradict one another. Moreover, the way we eat changes as we learn more, come to know ourselves better, and adapt to the evolving circumstances of our lives. Being aware of the New Four Food Groups and keeping them in mind as the foundation, if not the totality, of the way you eat does a couple of things. First, it's nutrition insurance. Eating a lot of plant-based foods in pretty much their natural state gives you enough, but not too much, protein, carbohydrate, and fat, as well as a plethora of vitamins, minerals, and phytochemicals, those wondrous substances in fruits and vegetables shown to protect the body from certain types of cancer and other degenerative diseases.

In addition, because these foods contain a lot of fiber (in grains and beans), water (in fruits), or both (in vegetables), you can eat until you're full, lose weight as long as you need to lose weight, and not gain it back after that. Privation is hard to sustain, and these are foods you can eat in enough quantity that privation won't even come up. Being able to sit down for a meal and have plenty is a comfort every person deserves, regardless of body size. The New Four Food Groups, if you want to use them as a flexible guideline, can help make this possible.

HAVE A PREDICTABLE LIFESTYLE

It's comforting to return to a foundation of predictability when

you're bedazzled by too much freedom or too many choices.

"BORING IS GOOD," the cab driver told me on the way to the airport. "With boring, you'll never have a heart attack." No one who knows me would ever accuse me of carrying the banner for boredom, but there is much to be said for predictability, especially when you're making major changes.

Have a predictable lifestyle. Eat at around the same time every day. Have a bedtime and a waking time, even if you sleep in on the weekends. Pay your bills on the first and the fifteenth or on some other schedule that works for you so you don't have to worry about what's been paid and what you may have forgotten. Shop for groceries on Friday after work or so early Saturday morning that you beat the crowds. Take yoga on Tuesday, a spinning class Thursday, and a walk in the park Sunday afternoon.

Won't this be dull? Sometimes. But that doesn't mean you'll be dull. You'll be functioning. It may seem contradictory that in this part of *Fit from Within* I am encouraging you to have predictability and in other parts I encourage you to have adventures.

They actually go hand in glove, with predictability as the base for adventures to rest on. It's like designing a one-of-a-kind house full of innovative features yet making certain that it's built on a strong foundation.

With a foundation of predictability supporting your life, you have standards in place. You can make exceptions, amendments, and alterations, but those standards stay put as your base of operations. It's reassuring to return to them when you're bedazzled by too much freedom or too many choices. Then, when the opportunity to do something extraordinary comes along, you'll be able to say, "Sure," because your passport is current, there's money in the bank, you have sick days saved up, and you're on good enough terms with your mother that she'll tend to your mail and your plants while you're off doing this extraordinary thing.

Give yourself the safety of a predictable schedule. You aren't married to it, but it will give you security. And it will be there for you when you need it. In a balanced life the mundane and the magical partner and dance. Don't be afraid of the former. Without it, the latter may never make it to the dance floor.

GROW SOMETHING TO EAT

⌒

"I start with the proposition that eating is an agricultural act."

—WENDELL BERRY

AT A FESTIVAL CELEBRATING small farmers and locally grown foods, I came upon an essay called "The Pleasures of Eating" by farmer, poet, and novelist Wendell Berry. In it he writes, "I start with the proposition that eating is an agricultural act." As one for whom eating had so often been an act of desperation or rebellion, I was taken with this simple sentence and read it over and over again.

I don't believe it's possible to understand eating as an agricultural act until you eat something you've grown yourself. So think about it: grow a garden. If you don't have a yard, grow tomatoes in a window box. If you don't have a window, grow sprouts on your kitchen counter.

I'm not a big gardener myself. It's hard for me to classify kneeling in the dirt, communing with crawling things, and pulling weeds in the hot sun as amusement. Nevertheless, I am grateful that I have gardened and that I've seen the wonder of seeds becoming plants that produce flowers and turn into tomatoes and peppers and so much zucchini that I'm convinced it's God's favorite vegetable. In having borne witness to this seasonal miracle, I can no longer look at food in the cavalier fashion I once did. I have a respect for it and for the people who grow it that was lacking before.

You can develop some of this respect (and not get dirt under your nails) by shopping at farmers' markets and talking to the farmers. They're rarer than celebrities these days and often far more interesting. I find farmers' markets in city settings especially engaging. I like the juxtaposition of concrete and steel with parsley and peaches and pumpkins. It's like wearing a lace blouse with jeans—startling and enticing at the same time.

You can also get farm-fresh food delivered to your door or a nearby drop-off spot from a Community Supported Agriculture project through which you actually buy shares in a farm for the season. Your dividends come in what the farm produces.

I did this one year when there was a drought in our area. Early on, a husband-and-wife team brought a weekly bounty of leaf lettuce and arugula and June's first berries from their small farm, but as summer wore on the baskets weren't as full and the vegetables not as attractive. By August the farmers could only offer apples—there was enough groundwater to nourish the roots of a tree—and eggs and the flavored vinegars they'd made to sell but gave to the shareholders instead because they didn't want to let us down. I'd been aware of droughts in past years, but not until that year did I really comprehend what lack of rain meant. It affected me because I owned a piece of the farm.

You can also take weekend drives to a pick-your-own orchard in the country. You'll learn the agility it takes to reach just the apple you're after and how much delicacy is required to harvest a raspberry. At the very least, buy produce that isn't wrapped in cellophane. Touch it. Know what you're getting. Eat more food that's fresh than frozen or canned. If you're going to eat the fresh stuff, you have to be involved with it—washing it, trimming it, peeling it. You're forced to spend enough time with it that you get the message: this is nature. And it's going to go into your body and quite literally become part of who you are. Most days this is as close to a miracle as we're going to get.

When you get a feel for food—what it really is, where it comes from, how extraordinary it is that the earth keeps producing for all the life forms that live here—you develop a reverence about it. And you won't have to eat so much of it to feel full and satisfied and at peace with the way things are.

93

Drink Water Until It Becomes Your Beverage of Choice

Once you start drinking it, you'll start liking it.

IT HAS BEEN SUGGESTED that the obesity epidemic may in part be a dehydration crisis: we're thirsty, but we think we're hungry, so instead of drinking water, we eat more food. There certainly could be something to this theory, because most Americans not only don't drink enough water but dehydrate themselves with caffeine and alcohol and by flying in planes, baking in saunas, and playing weekend warrior without replenishing lost fluids.

Drinking ample water can be a great friend to long-term weight loss because it assuages false hunger; it fulfills the brain's need for water, which we can mistake for a desire for sugar; and it makes us look and feel better, so taking care of ourselves proceeds more naturally.

Our choice of beverages is so vast that water has become an acquired taste (or an acquired *nontaste*, I should say). People who routinely drink coffee, tea, soda, beer, wine, mixed drinks, fruit drinks, and canned and bottled juices to the exclusion of water start to regard water as boring. Hearing advice like "You need to drink approximately sixty-four ounces of water every day" can make you feel like you've time-warped to eighth-grade hygiene class. It sounds like one more thing to do that almost nobody does, right up there with flossing and getting your tires rotated and cleaning off the refrigerator coils.

The suggestion to drink plenty of water, though, isn't just an idle "should" made up by some ogre who doesn't want you to enjoy life. Every chemical reaction that takes nutrients and makes them into energy requires a water molecule. Some people are able to lose weight simply by drinking more water, because that alone ramps up those chemical reactions so the entire system works more efficiently.

Besides, *moist* people look good. If you're dehydrated—and if you wait to drink water until you feel thirsty, you're nearly there—you will look older than you need to. You won't seem as firm and taut as you lose weight, even if you exercise. Your skin tone—face and body—just won't be there, regardless of how much you spend on creams and lotions. Dark circles under your eyes will be more pronounced, and so will any lines and crinkles. (You want the ones that give you character, not the ones that show up because you've inadvertently turned your body into a desert.)

Some real-life ways to drink more water include:

- *Keep pitchers of water with sliced lemon in your fridge and on your desk.* You'll see it, so you'll drink it, and the lemon makes it taste like something.

- *Ease yourself off colas and sweetened sodas with flavored sparkling water.* Sometimes just having that little bit of fizz makes the transition easier for a confirmed soda drinker.

- *Carry a half-liter bottle of water with you wherever you go.* If you have a bottle of water with you, you're less likely to pick up a can of soda. Buy them by the six-pack if that's what it takes; otherwise, refill the bottle from your own pure water source at home.

- *Start choosing water instead of other beverages until it becomes a habit.* Fancy restaurants will bring you a chilled bottle of San Pellegrino as if it were fine champage, and street vendors, quickie marts, and most movie theaters now sell water, too. (If you're offended by the idea of paying for water, remember that you'd be paying for the Pepsi or the iced latté anyway, and water is something you really need.)

- *When someone asks if you'd like a drink, request water.* And when someone asks if you'd like water, say yes.

- *In winter, sip warm water, with lemon or on its own.* Herbal teas like licorice, hibiscus, and chamomile can count as water, too. Look for lovely blends at your supermarket or natural foods store, and order them at restaurants when the server asks if you want coffee after dinner.

As one who formerly avoided plain, ordinary water (maybe I thought it would give me—heaven forbid—a plain, ordinary life), I can tell you that once you start drinking it, you'll start liking it. It's like recovering the ability to enjoy strawberries when you thought they needed shortcake, or apples when they're not in pie. Pure and simple has its own appeal.

94

Safeguard Your Health

When you reach a high level of health, or even when you're on

the road to it, the very process of living becomes a joy.

IF YOU NEED TO LOSE WEIGHT, doing so should improve your health. To keep up the good work, safeguard your health in all ways: regular medical checkups, rest, exercise, stress management, curtailed sun exposure, washing your hands before meals and brushing your teeth afterward—all the ho-hum stuff that is far more necessary than interesting.

Take exercise, for example. In spite of all the health clubs and athletic shoes and sports bras in this country, do you know what percentage of Americans exercise at least twenty minutes three times a week? Fifteen percent. Fifteen! If the weather person says there's a 15 percent chance of rain, you leave your umbrella at home. The fact that 85 percent of Americans aren't exercising tells me that most of us don't believe we're subject of the laws of nature. But like it or not, nature has the upper hand. Taking care of yourself can't guarantee a lifetime of perfect health, but it can surely hedge your bets.

This degree of health isn't just feeling well enough that you can't call in sick today. It is instead such a heightened sense of well-being that your mind and spirit get the spin-off. It's nearly impossible to have a negative attitude when you are supremely healthy. Let me fully acknowledge that I am not always this healthy. I get lazy sometimes, or I don't replenish the energy I give to work, family, and life's glittering diversions. But when I put my health at the top of my to-do list, it's not long before I feel on top of the world.

When you build a body out of the healthiest food, the healthiest environment, the healthiest lifestyle, and the healthiest attitudes you know of, it's like moving into a mansion from a tar-paper shack. At this level of health, or even on the road to it, the very process of living becomes a joy, and abusing yourself in any way becomes just about impossible.

BE IN THIS FOR THE LONG HAUL

Your inner life has to expand, or the outer expression

of it will revert back to default setting: the easy, the dependable,

the two scoops with extra whipped cream.

IF YOU WANT ONLY A different body, and not a different way of life, you can't expect the body changes to last, because there will be nothing to sustain them. In other words, you can't just lose weight and go back to business as usual without becoming overweight as usual. This has to be for the long haul.

Things will change, of course. You may need firmer boundaries in the beginning if you're just finding your way back from having no boundaries at all. At first you'll need to give more thought to eating well and avoiding foods that cause you trouble. Eventually you'll eat well because that's what you do, and you'll stay away from foods you'd rather not eat simply because you would rather not eat them.

Being in this for the long haul does not mean that you will have to worry about a food and weight problem for the rest of your life. If you do the mental and spiritual work required to become fit from within, you won't have a food and weight problem to worry about. Still, your continued freedom depends on altered attitudes. Your inner life has to expand, or the outer expression of it will revert back to default setting: the easy, the dependable, the two scoops with extra whipped cream.

Looking back with a perspective of eighteen years, I can tell you that I am rarely concerned about food or my weight today, but this was a long time coming. For a while—I don't know how long; as long as it takes—changing your thinking and living patterns has to be the most important thing in your life. Once this importance is etched in your psyche, you'll have it to draw on. You won't even realize it, but it will be there silently and unobtrusively, ready to protect you if necessary, like a smoke detector or a burglar alarm.

I've been thin for a long time, but I was fat longer. I appreciate what I have, but I don't take my good fortune for granted. Rather than holding me back or infringing on my freedom, this is actually a blessing. Otherwise a person like me—and you, too, maybe—could gain ten pounds without realizing what happened and then become so discouraged that the other twenty or fifty or one hundred pounds return with the force of an incoming tide. I'm in this for the long haul. If you want to be at peace with food and your body for the rest of your life, you'll be in it for the long haul, too.

96

BECOME FLEXIBLE

~

Flexibility means putting life ahead of food.

OF COURSE IT TAKES a certain amount of vigilance to lose excess weight and never regain it. That's why we've talked about eating real food, sticking pretty much with three meals a day, and much of the time ordering the small size. Still, if you want to make it through the rest of your life fit, healthy, and reasonably serene, you have to be somewhat flexible. This flexibility is largely what separates fly-by-night dieters from men and women who release excess weight for good. While the dieters are making everyone uncomfortable with their special foods and portion scales and complaints to the waiter, the people who have this down can usually make do with what is available. Minimal fuss.

For example, a useful parameter for me has been to eat what's on the plate, and when it's gone, that's it. Then I traveled to China, where the custom is to give every diner a tiny plate and present one course at a time for an hour or more. My "fill your plate and quit" tactic wouldn't help at all. I was uncomfortable because I depended on that strategy. To regain my comfortable relationship with food during those six weeks in China, however, I had to be flexible and do something different—in this case, have a modest amount of each course and trust I'd get enough. I always did.

Flexibility also means putting life ahead of food. A while back my teenage daughter, Adair, was juggling dozens of decisions that would impact her future. When she was finally willing to talk to me about all this, she said, "Let's go for potatofuls at the Corner Restaurant." The Corner Restaurant is a diner near our house in Kansas City, and the potatoful is Adair's favorite breakfast—fried potatoes with a choice of additions ranging from spinach to salsa to Greek olives.

I don't like fried potatoes, or fried anything for that matter. Even when my eating was as bad as it got, I didn't care much for greasy food. That Saturday morning, though, having a potatoful with Adair at the Corner Restaurant was the most important thing I could do. My body can deal with having fried potatoes every now and then, and being flexible about food that day gave me the chance to become closer to my daughter.

You might say, "Well, that's okay for you: you've already lost weight." It doesn't matter. Even if I were still losing weight, the chance for a tête-à-tête with a young woman who all too soon would not be a daily part of my life was far more precious than the extra quarter pound I might have lost that week. Flexibility helps us get the order right: life first, people first, food and weight somewhere down the list.

97

WATCH OUT FOR
"I'M A WHOLE NEW ME"

Never forget who you are or where you came from.

YOU'VE LOST WEIGHT. Congratulations. You did something difficult and important for yourself. But you're not a "whole new you." You're yourself with a smaller body. You've made some important changes in your lifestyle and, if this is going to last, in your thought processes, but you haven't joined the Witness Protection Program. You're still you.

The "whole new me" myth causes many people who lose weight to go out and have midlife crises—even if they're seventy. Or twenty-five. They want to make up for all they have presumably missed. This is a natural response, but it can go too far.

People who have suffered a lot from being heavy sometimes put too much stock in being thin. They expect the compliments to last (they won't), and they expect the world to be endlessly impressed by their accomplishment (it isn't). These folks are headed for disappointment, because the "world"—that illusive, collective "they" who can seem to hold such sway over us—

97

WATCH OUT FOR "I'M A WHOLE NEW ME"

Never forget who you are or where you came from.

YOU'VE LOST WEIGHT. Congratulations. You did something difficult and important for yourself. But you're not a "whole new you." You're yourself with a smaller body. You've made some important changes in your lifestyle and, if this is going to last, in your thought processes, but you haven't joined the Witness Protection Program. You're still you.

The "whole new me" myth causes many people who lose weight to go out and have midlife crises—even if they're seventy. Or twenty-five. They want to make up for all they have presumably missed. This is a natural response, but it can go too far.

People who have suffered a lot from being heavy sometimes put too much stock in being thin. They expect the compliments to last (they won't), and they expect the world to be endlessly impressed by their accomplishment (it isn't). These folks are headed for disappointment, because the "world"—that illusive, collective "they" who can seem to hold such sway over us—

236

doesn't think there is any excuse for being fat in the first place. The world expects us to do our jobs, pay our taxes, raise our kids, and get on with things. People with whole-new-me syndrome, however, are waiting for their crown and scepter. When these don't come, they can act out in some silly ways and some sad ones.

If you find yourself buying clothes with money you don't have, or living a twenty-something lifestyle with a forty-something ID, or dating men (or women) you don't particularly like just because they're "interested," you may be suffering from *whole new me*. If your ego gets out of hand and you start to feel that the rules that govern ordinary people don't apply to you, take remedial action. Blow up a picture of yourself at your top weight and hang it inside the door of your closet or medicine cabinet. The person in that photograph is you as much as the fashion plate who looked back at you from the mirror this morning. Never forget who you are or where you came from.

See yourself clearly. Visit somebody who knew you when you were ten. Sign up for ladle duty at a soup kitchen or tutor an underprivileged kid. Get things straight: you are a healthier, more attractive, and hopefully wiser person than you were some weeks or months ago. And as you continue to enrich your spiritual self, your life will unfold in ways you may have only dreamed of. Splendid. Now do something loving. Do something generous. Do something that makes a difference.

BE KIND TO YOURSELF

ON DIFFICULT DAYS

To keep from turning to food, it is imperative that you recognize

the difference between a bad day and a futile life.

NAVIGATORS HAVE TO deal with rough seas, pilots with choppy air, and everybody with bad days. You get through them by going through them. The challenge for someone concerned with healthier eating and stable weight is to go through them without extra food. To do this, you first have to resign yourself to the fact that difficult days are the periodic lot of every person on earth, even the ones whose lives seem idyllic.

The next step is to remind yourself as often as necessary that, in almost every case, such times are temporary. Chronic overeaters tend to see every difficulty—a quarrel, a pimple, a traffic ticket—as permanent. To keep from turning to food, it is imperative that you recognize the difference between a bad day and a futile life. Once you realize that you're having the former and not the latter, you can take the opportunity to treat yourself exceptionally well during inevitable hard times. This is when you can best learn how to be gentle with yourself and practice this gentleness when it means the most.

If bad days were distinct and discrete and didn't have the annoying habit of clumping together, they wouldn't be so hard to deal with. It's when you get a spate of them that you need the patience of Job to keep going, take care of yourself, and not swallow anything suspect. During stretches that seem bleak, either because unfortunate things are happening or because good things aren't, you have to put something bright into each day, even if you'd rather be good and miserable and have done with it.

Treat yourself the way you would treat a child you love very much. With that child, you'd be patient and kind. You would give in when that was appropriate and say no when it wasn't. You wouldn't push the child beyond his capabilities, but you'd help him grow every chance you got. If you can do that for yourself, you can get through tough times without making them worse through self-inflicted pain.

This is when it's good to be philosophical. Spiritual literature is likely to speak to you more clearly now than at any other time, and you're apt to find in even familiar stories and passages insights that are new to you. Reading mythology and poetry can be helpful, too: these are descriptions of the myriad experiences people go through, and chances are something you read will address what you're going through now. Seeing a counselor or a spiritual director can be profitable during these intervals when you have the task of acknowledging what is wrong in your life without losing sight of all that is right there.

Difficult times come in two basic forms: the annoying and the tragic. Ninety-nine percent of our difficulties are in the annoying category. When you realize this, you'll worry less, find more joy in the midst of the junk, and be able to count your blessings, even when it would feel really good to count your tribulations instead.

When you experience a genuine tragedy—and no one that I know of gets through life without at least a few—you have to trust that this is when a Higher Power can really be there for you. Sometimes people who have confronted a life-threatening illness, grieved the death of a loved one, or gone through a grueling divorce talk about the uncanny peacefulness they felt at times while this was going on. They felt pain, of course, but there was also a sense of protection, as if they were living not only their ordinary life with a struggle at its center, but a larger life of greater meaning and inexplicable joy. If we can access something this amazing during the worst of times, surely we can get through the rest of it.

99

Develop an Attitude
of Gratitude

~

Pie in the sky? Maybe. But pie in the sky won't make you fat

or clog your arteries like pie on the earth did.

Have an attitude of gratitude. Don't skip this because you've heard it before and it's a silly rhyme you needlepointed on a pillow in 1998. Without an attitude of gratitude, renewable every day, you are a ripe candidate for self-pity, and that is often the prelude to a convenience store sweep. Head it off at the pass with your grateful feelings.

A helpful exercise is to write ten things you're grateful for every morning (okay, night people: evening) in your journal or day planner. If you get discouraged, frustrated, or overwhelmed during the day, write ten more. Big things, little things, it doesn't matter. Any Creator who could come up with whales and mice and give them basically the same organs is obviously not concerned with size. The perceived size of your blessings probably doesn't count for much either.

A gratitude list of mine might start as follows:

1. I am grateful that my husband believes in my dreams.

2. I am grateful that my daughter was cast in the play she auditioned for.

3. I am grateful that the sun is shining today.

4. I am grateful that I feel so good physically.

5. I am grateful to be writing in a lovely little coffeehouse, and I'm grateful that they're playing music that doesn't annoy me.

Once you write ten, your day looks different. Your life feels better. Your world seems more accommodating. On tough mornings, the ones when getting out of bed seems like a really bad idea, you may want to make your list mentally before your feet touch the floor. It can get your priorities in order almost instantly.

When gratitude moves in, happiness usually comes along. If you start every day by making a gratitude list, whether on paper or in your head, your brain comes to realize that you'll need entries for your list. It then makes note of the good things that happen to you during the day. Many of these you might otherwise have brushed aside, not realizing they were gifts from life as surely as if they'd come wrapped with shiny paper and curly ribbon. As you get into the gratitude groove, you'll feel pleasant sensations more acutely. You'll notice beauty you might have overlooked before. Eventually you'll find it challenging to keep your list down to ten.

Pie in the sky? Maybe. But pie in the sky won't make you fat or clog your arteries like pie on the earth did. Besides, gratitude is healing and rejuvenating. It puts a refreshing spin on things and changes the way you interpret your life. Eventually you may even be grateful for having had a weight problem, because in finding your way out of it you grew in compassion and learned to trust.

100

Allow Yourself to Grow and Change

~

Not only are your life circumstances different than they

used to be, but the very cells that make up your body

are different from the ones you had before.

I WILL NEVER FORGET the first breakfast I ate after my last binge. It was November 1983, at a riverside diner in St. Charles, Illinois, some fifty miles west of Chicago. I had an omelet, oozing with cheese, pumpernickel toast with margarine, orange juice, and coffee. The meal was particularly memorable because I took one of the pieces of toast to the river and fed it to the Canada geese who had recently arrived, believing that for yet one more winter Chicago could pass for "south."

Even one day earlier, when I was a practicing compulsive eater, no goose would have gotten a crumb of my breakfast. But this day was different. I was onto something. The hurt of turning to food and then having it turn on me had become so acute that I let it go. I didn't know if I would live my life fat or thin, but I knew I had to get out from under. At the insistence of a friend who had been down this road before, I had asked God or the Goddess or whoever was up there (or in here—I wasn't really sure) to take away the hideous cravings, and that morning, the only one that mattered, He or She or It came through. And He or She or It still does.

Many other things are different. For instance, these days I seldom drink coffee but really like tea, especially the green kind that just might cure everything. I no longer eat cheese omelets, and I don't use margarine. As a result my cholesterol level, HDL and LDL, homocysteine, and triglycerides put me in the cum laude category. Nevertheless, that breakfast, that day, was just right. I was doing the best I knew how with the resources I had, and it was the beginning of a grander life than I knew then was possible.

Allow yourself to grow and change. Base your food choices and your life choices on the highest and best you know today. As long as this works for you, let it. If you learn something that seems better, try it. If it turns out not to be all it promised, let it fall away.

You may be one of the countless people who lost weight on some diet or other, gained it back, and tried to lose it again on the same diet. It ought to work. It did before. In practice, though, the second (or third or fourth) time around is usually an abject failure because, even though the diet hasn't changed, you have. What worked when you lived with a roommate in a college dorm probably won't when you're married with a couple of toddlers in tow. The diet you lost weight on last year when it was new and exciting may not come through for you now, when it seems old and restrictive. You may have lost weight in the past out of sheer willpower, willpower that has now grown impotent.

This is to be expected: not only are your life circumstances different than they used to be, but the very cells that make up your body are different from the ones you had before. And if your overeating has an addictive component, this is progressive. Left unchecked, it gets worse. It's not your fault. You just need more now than the diet that once seemed like a godsend. Allow yourself to grow and change. Trust that you know yourself better now than you ever have. Let this knowledge work in your favor.

101

JUST KEEP MOVING FORWARD

Trust that you'll be taken care of and expect that you'll make

good choices. Good is good enough. Perfect is a setup.

CHANGING FROM THE inside out requires a refurbishing of both lifestyle and personality. This is why the suggestions in *Fit from Within* deal not only with eating and exercise but with myriad aspects of your being, how you see yourself, how you relate to the world around you, and how much help you are willing to accept from whatever Higher Power is part of your sense of things.

In spite of all these aspects coming together to change your relationship with food, your body, and your life, the only thing with which you have to concern yourself today is moving forward, even if that sometimes involves taking a step back. Do whatever you need to do to keep food that isn't right for you from passing your lips. You don't even have to think about doing that forever. Today is enough.

Use the techniques you've learned from this book, and what you have stored in your own well of wisdom, to eat as sanely, as healthfully, and as fearlessly as you can at appropriate times from morning till night. Keep this book with you as long as you need it. Have it in the kitchen, in your car, in your desk at work. Know that you can pull it out, open it up, and the part you read will be the part you need. You're working hard to bring yourself and your life into harmony with universal laws. I think you can certainly expect a perk as minor as opening a book to the right page.

You can also expect to get what you need, including the degree of transformation necessary to make the most of your life. Perfection does not exist in this world, and sometimes you will eat too much. You may not even realize it until you stand up and your belt feels tight or your stomach feels fuller than you'd like. This is part of the process. It's how you learn what enough is—enough lunch, enough weight loss, enough attention given to your belt and your stomach. Set reasonable parameters for yourself. Go into this day with the honest intention of eating the way you would if you loved yourself as much as God does.

For me, saying a sincere prayer is helpful, both before embarking on the day and for framing meals. One overeater with long-standing freedom from the vexation told me she approaches menus, salad bars, and buffets with the simple phrase "Okay, God, you're on." It has yet to fail her. Trust the God of your understanding without reservation, and one day you will discover that you're able to trust yourself, too. Trust that you'll be taken care of and expect that you'll make good choices. Good is good enough. Perfect is a setup. Without being perfect, you can do just fine today. And that's a pretty good start on forever.

RESOURCES AND
RECOMMENDED READING

CHAPTER 3. "Include a Spiritual Component." People who explore their spirituality find books and writers that, as the Quakers say, "speak to their condition." I'd like to recommend two, each quite different from the other but both respectful of the myriad paths humans take to find meaning. *Spirituality for Dummies,* by Sharon Janis (Hungry Minds, 2000), uses the lighthearted style of the Dummies series to get across profound concepts. And Aldous Huxley's classic of the inner life, *The Perennial Philosophy* (HarperCollins, reissue edition, 1990), explores such topics as "Faith," "Self-Knowledge," and "Spiritual Experience" from the standpoint of the underlying wisdom all spiritual traditions share.

CHAPTER 6. "Focus on Living a Quality Life." Living your dreams and making a difference equals a quality life. (It also combats any problems that might arise from getting caught up in the glory of having your jeans fit.) Inspire yourself by reading about people who have done it in *Living Big: Embrace Your Passion and Leap into an Extraordinary Life*, by Pam Grout (Conari Press, 2001).

CHAPTER 9. "Eat Like a Healthy Human Being." I cannot recommend highly enough Dr. Andrew Weil's *Eating Well for Optimum Health: The Essential Guide to Bringing Health and Pleasure Back to Eating* (Quill, 2001). After reading this book, you'll know everything there is to know about the importance of whole foods, not only for being healthy but for living the good life.

CHAPTER 13. "Walk More." *The Spirited Walker: Fitness Walking for Clarity, Balance, and Spiritual Connection*, by Carolyn Scott Kortge (HarperSanFrancisco, 1998), is a lovely introduction to walking for body and soul.

CHAPTER 15. "Write What You Eat and Keep on Writing." If you're not used to keeping a journal, or if you would like to work with a guided journal targeted specifically at getting fit and feeling better about yourself, I wrote *Body Confident: A Guided Journal for Losing Weight and Feeling Great* (Walking Stick Press, 2001) just for you. It's filled with prompts to get you started writing and lots of lovely blank pages for you to express yourself.

CHAPTER 20. "If You Have a Serious Problem, Take Serious Action." Overeaters Anonymous uses the same twelve-step program as Alcoholics Anonymous, and it can be a godsend. If you live in a good-sized city, there should be a listing for Overeaters Anonymous in the white pages (try both business and residential). Otherwise, visit the website for the OA World Service, www.overeatersanonymous.org; or write to Overeaters Anonymous, P.O. Box 44020, Rancho Rio, NM 87124.

CHAPTER 21. "Eat Enough." For visual evidence of how you really can eat enough and still lose weight, see *Dr. Shapiro's Picture Perfect Weight Loss: The Visual Program for Permanent Weight Loss*, by Howard M. Shapiro, M.D. (Rodale Press, 2000).

CHAPTER 22. "Wear Clothes You Like in Your Current Size." Clothes can be fun, whatever your size. They became even more fun for me after I read *Secrets of a Fashion Therapist: What You Can Learn Behind the Dressing Room Door*, by Bergdorf Goodman personal shopper Betty Halbreich with Sally Wadyka and Jeffrey Fulvimari (Cliff Street Books, 2000).

CHAPTER 24. "Lighten Up." A delightful little book that has helped me lighten up and enjoy more moments is Leslie Levine's *Ice Cream for Breakfast: If You Follow All the Rules, You'll Miss Half the Fun* (Contemporary Books, 2001).

CHAPTER 29. "Give Thanks Before and After Meals." My favorite collection of table graces is *Graces: Prayers and Poems for Everyday Meals and Special Occasions*, June Cotner, ed. (HarperSanFrancisco, 1994). There are 133 of them from a variety of cultures, arranged by theme.

CHAPTER 36. "Get Down and Dirty with Life." I am so passionate about being passionate that I wrote a book about it: *Creating a Charmed Life: Sensible, Spiritual Secrets Every Busy Woman Should Know* (HarperSanFrancisco, 1999). If you'd like to make a magical life out of the one you've got, this will help.

CHAPTER 38. "Groom Yourself like a Racehorse." A lot of books about beauty and grooming are unrealistic and silly. One that is instead useful for real people and beautifully illustrated as well is *K.I.S.S. Guide to Beauty*, by Stephanie Pederson (DK Publishing, Inc., 2001). I liked it so much I wrote the foreword.

CHAPTER 43. "Learn to Cook—or to Cook Differently." If you're in the market for a cookbook, look for health-promoting recipes that are easy enough to follow that you don't have to graduate from the Culinary Institute of America to make dinner. The ones I'm using a lot these days are *The Vegetarian 5-Ingredient Gourmet*, by Nava Atlas (Broadway Books, 2001); *Everyday Cooking with Dr. Dean Ornish*, by Dean Ornish, M.D., Janet Kessel Fletcher, and Helen Roe, contributors (HarperCollins, 1997); and *The Peaceful Palate*, by Jennifer Raymond (The Book Publishing Company, 1996).

CHAPTER 45. "Get All Six Tastes in Every Meal." This is a concept from the Indian healing system of Ayurveda, a system brilliantly explored and clearly explained by Bri Maya Tiwari in *The Path of Practice: A Woman's Book of Healing with Food, Breath, and Sound* (Ballantine, 2000).

CHAPTER 47. "Watch Naturally Thin People." I enjoyed reading *The Seven Secrets of Slim People*, by Vicki Hansen, M.S.W., and Shawn Goodman (Hay House, 1997; HarperPaperbacks, 1998). Its message is that dieting can make you fatter and it makes sense to adopt the attitudes of the naturally slim.

CHAPTER 50. "Be Careful with Caffeine." In switching from coffee and colas to tea, I both cut back on caffeine and discovered the fascinating lore and rituals that surround tea drinking around the world. If you have an interest in taking tea with pizzazz, I recommend *Tea with Friends*, by Elizabeth Knight (Storey Books, 1998).

CHAPTER 51. "Tap into Your Courage." An acutely pragmatic read to help you draw on your courage in business and in life is *What's Holding You Back?: Thirty Days to Having the Courage and Confidence to Do What You Want, Meet Whom You Want, and Go Where You Want*, by Sam Horn (St. Martin's Press, 1997).

CHAPTER 53. "Be Willing to Change at the Desire Level." A lovely book that looks at overeating as a disorder of desire and uses Buddhist principles, gently presented, to deal with it, is *The Zen of Eating: Ancient Answers to Modern Weight Problems*, by Ronna Kabatznick (Perigee, 1998).

CHAPTER 55. "Discover Yoga." *Yoga Mind & Body*, compiled by the Sivananda Yoga Vedanta Center (DK Publishing, Inc., 1998), is the book I give all my friends who express an interest in yoga. It's clear and complete, and the color photos put it in a league of its own. The book also addresses the yogic dietary philosophy and moral code.

You may also wish to visit the website of YogaPlus International, conceived by yoga instructor Panchali Null to make yoga more accessible to heavier women and men: www.yogaplusinternational.com. (I've taken class with Panchali, and she's top-notch.)

CHAPTER 57. "Meditate." A book I've loved spending time with is *Meditation Secrets for Women: Discovering Your Passion, Pleasure, and Inner Peace*, by Camille Maurine and Lorin Roche, Ph.D. (HarperSanFrancisco, 2001). (Men: I think you would like this, too; it's awfully good.)

CHAPTER 61. "Shop the Produce Section First." A practical and motivational book to help you incorporate more fruits and vegetables into your diet—and feel healthier in your body, mind, and spirit—is *A Fresh Start: Sure-Fire Tips & Recipes to Accelerate Fat Loss & Restore Youthful Vitality*, by Susan Smith Jones (Celestial Arts, 2002).

CHAPTER 66. "Go Ahead and Have a Beautiful Face." My previous book, *Lit from Within: Tending Your Soul for Lifelong Beauty* (HarperSanFrancisco, 2001), is about bringing your inner beauty out so you become one of those people who light up a room, regardless of the size of your body or how old you are.

CHAPTER 71. "Learn to Wait." The inspiration for this chapter was Hermann Hesse's classic, *Siddhartha* (Bantam Classics, 1982, Hilda Rosner, translator), a story of the prince who became the Buddha.

CHAPTER 75. "Think and Speak Positively." My favorite book for keeping my thoughts elevated is *The Power of Positive Choices: Adding and Subtracting Your Way to a Great Life*, by Gail McMeekin, M.S.W. (Conari Press, 2001).

If you're interested in one-on-one coaching to "change your words, change your life," positive language specialist Elizabeth Cutting offers private consultations by phone. The theory is that the words we choose play a role in determining the quality of our lives. Contact her by E-mail at elizabeth@elizabethcutting.com.

CHAPTER 76. "Eschew Fast Food." *Fast Food Nation*, by Eric Schlosser (Houghton Mifflin Co., 2001), is a laudable piece of journalism that reads like a novel and has enough fascinating (and enlightening) information to steer you past fast-food places for a good long time.

CHAPTER 77. "Keep Things Simple." There are lots of books about simplifying your life, and I've read most of them. Especially enjoyable was *Seven Steps to Unclutter Your Life*, by Donna Smallin (Storey Books, 2000)—quick tips for life balance, stress reduction, more time, less mess.

CHAPTER 84. "Get Used to Sweating." Even a little exercise will pay handsome dividends, but if you're interested in getting in seriously good shape, the writings of Covert Bailey are classics in the field. His original *Fit or Fat*, which I read early in my recovery from overeating, helped me overcome a real aversion to exercise. The revised and updated edition of Bailey's original book is *The Ultimate Fit or Fat: Get in Shape and Stay in Shape with America's Best-Loved and Most Effective Fitness Teacher* (Houghton Mifflin, 2000).

CHAPTER 87. "Visit an Art Museum." The art book I mention in this chapter is Lawrence Gowing's *Paintings in the Louvre* (Stewart, Tabori, & Chang, 1987). It's not quite like a trip to Paris, but it can certainly make you want to take a trip to Paris.

You may also want to become familiar with the Real Women Project, designed to "unveil and celebrate the diverse beauty of women through

multi-media and the arts." Their website is www.realwomenproject
.com.

CHAPTER 90. "Meet the New Four Food Groups." Neal Barnard, M.D.,
the man who coined the term, is the author of *Food for Life: How the New
Four Food Groups Can Save Your Life* (Crown, 1994). His newest book,
*Turn Off the Fat Genes: The Revolutionary Guide to Taking Charge of the
Genes That Control Your Weight* (Crown, 2001), addresses how genetics
influence weight and ways to steer these factors in your favor.

CHAPTER 92. "Grow Something to Eat." Wendell Berry's "The Pleasures of Eating," to which I allude in this chapter, is one of many
thought-provoking essays in his book *What Are People For?* (North
Point Press, 1990). This book is also available in audio format. The combination of his well-chosen words and the soothing, down-on-the-farm
musicality of Berry's voice make listening a real treat.

If you're interested in learning more about Community Supported
Agriculture or locating a CSA farm in your area, visit the website of the
Bio-Dynamic Farming and Gardening Association, www.biodynam
ics.com, or write to them at P.O. Box 29135, San Francisco, CA 94129.

CHAPTER 98. "Be Kind to Yourself on Difficult Days." Father Paul
Keenan's *Good News for Bad Days: Living a Soulful Life* (Warner Books,
1999) offers simple, workable techniques for remembering the soul when
things go wrong.

To CONTACT THE AUTHOR, or to inquire about phone consultations or about booking her to speak for your organization, visit her website: www.victoriamoran.com.